"I've always contended that if we were more heavenly minded now, we could do more earthly good. Happily, in this brilliant devotional John and Kathy help you do this each day of your life. Rejoice! Heaven *is* about now and later! What a way to start your day."

Don Piper, *New York Times* bestselling author and speaker

"By nature and background I would typically be somewhat skeptical of a book like this. But knowing John and Kathy personally and understanding the type of research they did, I read this book with an open heart and mind. What you will read is . . . a glimpse. A peek through the edge of a pulled-back curtain, a thin place. Created for a perfect world, you and I get weary, and this book allows us the vision that restores our faith to not simply wait for the future but to live deeply and differently because of that future."

Nancy Ortberg, author of *Looking for God: An Unexpected Journey Through Tattoos, Tofu & Pronouns*

"As a physician who knows just how real heaven is, I congratulate Kathy and John on their ability to remind us of God's promises and bring the hope of heaven into daily life today through this inspirational and encouraging devotional."

Mary C. Neal, MD, author of *To Heaven and Back* and *7 Lessons from Heaven*

IMAGINE HEAVEN

Devotional

100 REFLECTIONS TO BRING
HEAVEN TO YOUR LIFE TODAY

JOHN BURKE
AND KATHY BURKE

BakerBooks

a division of Baker Publishing Group
Grand Rapids, Michigan

Published by Baker Books
a division of Baker Publishing Group
PO Box 6287, Grand Rapids, MI 49516-6287
www.bakerbooks.com

Printed in the United States of America

Library of Congress Cataloging-in-Publication Data
Names: Burke, John, 1963– author.
Title: Imagine heaven devotional : 100 reflections to bring heaven to your life today / John Burke and Kathy Burke.
Description: Grand Rapids : Baker Publishing Group, 2018.
Identifiers: LCCN 2018009829 | ISBN 9780801093623 (cloth)
Subjects: LCSH: Heaven—Christianity—Prayers and devotions. | Future life—Christianity—Prayers and devotions. | Near-death experiences—Religious aspects—Christianity—Prayers and devotions.
Classification: LCC BT848 .B779 2018 | DDC 236/.24—dc23
LC record available at https://lccn.loc.gov/2018009829

Unless otherwise indicated, Scripture quotations are from the Holy Bible, New International Version®. NIV®. Copyright © 1973, 1978, 1984, 2011 by Biblica, Inc.™ Used by permission of Zondervan. All rights reserved worldwide. www.zondervan.com

Scripture quotations labeled GNT are from the Good News Translation—Second Edition. Copyright © 1992 by American Bible Society. Used by permission.

Scripture quotations labeled MSG are from THE MESSAGE. Copyright © by Eugene H. Peterson 1993, 1994, 1995, 1996, 2000, 2001, 2002. Used by permission of NavPress. All rights reserved. Represented by Tyndale House Publishers, Inc.

Scripture quotations labeled NASB are from the New American Standard Bible®, copyright © 1960, 1962, 1963, 1968, 1971, 1972, 1973, 1975, 1977, 1995 by The Lockman Foundation. Used by permission. (www.Lockman.org)

Scripture quotations labeled NLT are from the Holy Bible, New Living Translation, copyright © 1996, 2004, 2015 by Tyndale House Foundation. Used by permission of Tyndale House Publishers, Inc., Carol Stream, Illinois 60188. All rights reserved.

Scripture quotations labeled NLV are from the New Life Version, copyright © 1969 by Christian Literature International.

This book contains original material as well as excerpts from *Imagine Heaven: Near-Death Experiences, God's Promises, and the Exhilarating Future That Awaits You* by John Burke (Baker Books, 2015).

Some names and details have been changed to protect the privacy of the individuals involved.

In keeping with biblical principles of creation stewardship, Baker Publishing Group advocates the responsible use of our natural resources. As a member of the Green Press Initiative, our company uses recycled paper when possible. The text paper of this book is composed in part of post-consumer waste.

22 23 24   7 6 5 4 3

This book is dedicated to those who courageously shared their stories of Heaven, trusting their sacred journeys would point people toward God and his relentless, amazing love and mercy available for all willing people.

Introduction

SINCE YOU HAVE BEEN RAISED to new life with Christ, set your sights on the realities of heaven, where Christ sits in the place of honor at God's right hand. Think about the things of heaven, not the things of earth" (Col. 3:1–2 NLT). That is the purpose of this devotional—to help us truly set our minds on the magnificent promises of Heaven, so that it will change how we live today.

But Christians often have a very poor view of Heaven. Too many imagine Heaven far less pleasing than earth, and as a result, they live their lives for what is temporal rather than what is eternal. Our desire in writing this devotional is to help you live today with awareness and confidence of your life's eternal value.

Heaven and near-death experiences (NDEs), where people died, were resuscitated, and claimed to have had a peek into the afterlife, have been a hot topic. Usually we are asked to just take a person's word for it. But I've never been one to gullibly believe every story of seeing Heaven. As a result, it took thirty-five years to write *Imagine Heaven*. Over that time, I studied close to one thousand near-death accounts (there are millions out there).

The Gallup Poll estimates that one out of every twenty-five people have had a near-death experience. After studying or interviewing so many people who had NDEs, amazing commonalities appeared across stories—intriguing, detailed descriptions by doctors, professors, commercial airline pilots, children, people from other countries—all giving different angles to what started to look like a similar picture.

During that same thirty-five-year time frame, I went from a career in engineering to becoming a pastor, and the more I studied the Christian Scriptures, on my own and in seminary, the more intriguing and confusing reading about NDEs became. Intriguing because so many of them described the picture of the afterlife found in the Scriptures; confusing because individual interpretations of their experiences could wildly vary and even seem at odds with the Scriptures.

After studying enough near-death experiences, I started to see the difference between what the people *reported* experiencing and the *interpretation* they might give to that experience based on cultural background or worldview. While interpretations vary, when evaluated together, the core elements of their testimonies point to what the Scriptures say. In fact, the more I studied, the more I realized that the picture Scripture paints of the exhilarating life to come is the common experience that many NDErs (near-death experiencers) describe.

In the book *Imagine Heaven*, I put together the evidence for the validity of NDEs. I show why so many skeptical medical doctors became convinced the afterlife is real because of what NDErs reported while out of their physical bodies, but still in the room where their resuscitation took place. I also show how their experience of the doorway of Heaven correlates with the amazing picture of the life to come painted in the Bible.

Imagine Heaven uses the stories of NDErs to help us imagine what the Bible describes. We believe the Bible should be the authority and framework for understanding Heaven and interpreting NDEs. We encourage you to read *Imagine Heaven* for a better understanding of the bigger biblical framework surrounding these stories and for answers to many of the questions commonly asked.

The *Imagine Heaven Devotional* has been written for personal application of the biblical promises of Heaven, in hopes of bringing Heaven's blessings to your life today. My wife, Kathy, has written one hundred inspirational daily reflections, filled with God's truth and wisdom, to encourage you as you go through the challenges of life here on earth.

Kathy and I have served as partners in ministry together for twenty-nine years, beginning as college pastors, to missionaries overseas, to founding and serving in Gateway Church in Austin for the past two decades. She has contributed significantly to all the books I've written. That is why I'm so excited to have you hear directly from her. Kathy has amazing gifts of encouragement and teaching that breathe life into everyone she encounters. In these devotionals based on my research, you will experience that same life-giving inspiration, affirmation of your immense value to God, and daily hope for living. In this devotional, you will be inspired by stories included in *Imagine Heaven* along with new stories, all from the perspective of the promises of God in the Bible.

We are told by the apostle Paul to imagine Heaven—to set our minds on the realities of Heaven, so that it changes how we live today. These daily reflections will help you set your mind on what God has promised in his Word and live with an eternal perspective, as you are reminded of the reality of Heaven's blessings by those who claim to have gotten a glimpse. We are praying that God uses this devotional to deeply encourage you and to help bring more of the peace and joy of Heaven into your life each day.

John Burke

1

No eye has seen, no ear has heard, and no mind has imagined what God has prepared for those who love him.

1 Corinthians 2:9 NLT

Captain Dale Black had always dreamed of being a pilot. As a young man, one fateful day, his plane lost power after takeoff and crashed into a 75-foot-high aviation monument at 135 miles per hour. Everyone died except Dale, who came back to tell about it. At first, Dale found himself suspended in midair, hovering over the wreckage of his body and the plane. Then he began traveling at a great speed, accompanied by two angelic escorts.

I was fast approaching a magnificent city, golden and gleaming among a myriad of resplendent colors. The light I saw was the purest I had ever seen. And the music was the most majestic, enchanting, and glorious I had ever heard. I was still approaching the city, but now I was slowing down. Like a plane making its final approach for landing. I knew instantly that this place was entirely and utterly holy. Don't ask me how I knew, I just knew. . . .

Below me lay the purest, most perfect grass, precisely the right length and not a blade that was bent or even out of place. It was the most vibrant green I had ever seen. If a color can be said to be alive, the green I saw was alive, slightly transparent and emitting light and life from within each blade. The iridescent grass stretched endlessly over gently rolling hills upon which were sprinkled the most colorful wild flowers, lifting their soft-petaled beauty skyward, almost as if they were a chorus of flowers caught up in their own way of praising God.

The fragrance that permeated heaven was so gentle and sweet, I almost didn't notice it amid all there was to see and hear. But as I looked at the delicate, perfect flowers and grass, I wanted to smell them. Instantly, I was aware of a gentle aroma. As I focused, I could tell the difference between the grass and the flowers, the trees and even the air. It was all so pure and intoxicating and blended together in a sweet and satisfying scent.

In the distance stood a range of mountains, majestic in appearance, as if they reigned over the entire landscape. These were not mountains you wanted to conquer; these were mountains you wanted to revere. . . . Next I heard the faint sound of water rushing in the distance. I couldn't see the water, but it sounded as if it were rivers cascading over a series of small waterfalls, creating music that was ever changing. . . .

[The city wall] stretched out to my left and right as far as I could see in both directions. . . . A powerful light permeated the wall, and you could see all the colors of the rainbow in it. Strangely, whenever I moved, the colors moved ever so slightly as if sensing my movement and making an adjustment.[1]

Hebrews 8:5 says that Moses's Tabernacle was "a copy and shadow of what is in heaven." All we love about this earth is merely a shadow of the greater reality to come!

Think about all we desire on earth: beautiful landscapes and homes in a picture-perfect setting, all the time in the world to be with the people we love, endless energy to experience all the things we enjoy, and opportunities to work on fun and challenging projects in line with our passions. Even though this life falls short, our desires for these things point to the Creator of every good gift, and our longings point to what Heaven will bring.

When you think about your dreams in life, start including more than just your earthly dream house, vacation, career, or lifestyle. Imagine also the beauty and excitement waiting for you in your eternal life to come, and prioritize what matters most—loving God and loving others. Today, fix your eyes on the prize God has for you that lasts forever.

> **Prayer:** *Dear God, thank you for every good gift you've given me to enjoy now, and I look forward to the eternal blessings I will enjoy forever in Heaven!*

2

Don't be afraid, for I am with you. Don't be discouraged, for I am your God. I will strengthen you and help you. I will hold you up with my victorious right hand.

Isaiah 41:10 NLT

D R. MARY NEAL, an orthopedic spine surgeon, was on a white-water kayak trip in Chile when she plunged over a waterfall. The nose of her kayak lodged between two boulders, trapping her beneath a cascading torrent of water.

I very quickly knew that I would likely die. At that point I completely surrendered the outcome to God's will. The moment I asked that God's will be done, I was immediately and very physically held by Christ and reassured that everything would be fine. . . . I love the water still but I'd always, always feared a drowning death. . . . but at no point did I ever have fear. I never felt air hunger. I never felt panic. I'm a spine surgeon. I certainly tried to do those things that would free me or free the boat, but I felt great. I felt more alive than I've ever felt.

The very moment I turned to Him, I was overcome with an absolute feeling of calm, peace, and of the very physical sensation of being held in someone's arms. . . . I knew with absolute certainty that I was being held and comforted by Jesus.

After fourteen minutes under water, Mary's body finally broke free from the kayak, and she experienced a feeling of release.

It felt as if I had finally shaken off my heavy outer layer, freeing my soul. . . . I was immediately greeted by a group of . . . people, spirits, beings. . . . I absolutely knew that they were there to welcome me and greet me and make me feel loved and comfortable. . . .

My arrival was joyously celebrated and a feeling of absolute love was palpable as these spiritual beings and I hugged, danced, and greeted each other. The intensity, depth, and purity of these feelings and sensations were far greater than I could ever describe with words and far greater than anything I have ever experienced on earth. . . .

I knew that I was going home. My eternal home. . . . I glimpsed back at the scene on the river bank. My body [which had now been recovered but "dead" for thirty minutes] looked like the shell of a comfortable old friend, and I felt warm compassion and gratitude for its use. . . . I heard them [friends kayaking with Mary] call to me and beg me to take a breath. I loved them and did not want them to be sad, so I asked my heavenly companions to wait while I returned to my body, lay down, and took a breath.[1]

Just imagine, the experience you fear most—the death of your earthly body—actually frees you in a way you never dreamed it could. How liberating to know that you have absolutely nothing to fear—not even death!

As 1 Corinthians 15:54–56 (NLT) promises, "Then, when our dying bodies have been transformed into bodies that will never die, this Scripture will be fulfilled: 'Death is swallowed up in victory. O death, where is your victory? O death, where is your sting?'" Death has no power over us, for our real lives will have just begun!

In the same way, there is nothing else to fear on earth, knowing Heaven is in store. No matter what insecurities you face, Jesus wants to walk with you every minute of every day to bring comfort and peace to your heart, to displace even your greatest fears imaginable.

Jesus is with you always! Whatever your fears may be, release them to him, for he is faithful. Fill your heart and mind with the confident assurance that you are eternally safe with Jesus by your side.

> **Prayer:** *Jesus, I surrender my fears that are holding me back from experiencing the joy you have for me. I trust in your promise to strengthen me and help me.*

3

I praise you because I am fearfully and wonderfully made; your works are wonderful; I know that full well.

Psalm 139:14

HANNAH GREW UP in a very abusive home as a child. She felt unloved, unwanted, and didn't have one happy memory. But at age fourteen, she was in a severe car accident. Her whole life replayed in seconds, and then she found herself in a place where she realized how unconditionally loved, valued, and beautiful she was in God's eyes:

I always said the same things in my mind over and over growing up: Why wouldn't God protect me from being abused? Didn't I love him enough, that he might help me like the people in the Bible? . . .

This time when I was thinking them to myself, . . . I was getting answers back. It was a male's voice. His voice was soothing and calming. . . . "Why won't God protect me?" I heard, "He will." I said, "He will?!!" He said, "Yes." With each answer, I could feel the weight of worry come off my spirit. . . .

I asked, "Why won't God stick up for me?" He told me the things I was dealing with were all temporary. I told him I didn't do all those things of which I was being accused. . . . He said, "I believe you." I said, "You do?" I can't tell you how great it felt to have someone believe me. . . .

I went through the rest of my thoughts. "I wish I were beautiful." I heard, "You are." I said, "I am?!" He said, "Yes." . . . I was thinking to myself that I've always wanted to be more beautiful than I thought I was. I thought about what he said for a while. . . . I was just so happy someone thought I was beautiful. I was overflowing with joy with each response. Still all the while, someone was holding me. . . .

I said, "I wish I was perfect." He said, "You are!" I said, "I am?!" He said, "Yes, you are." Well, I thought I must have been doing something wrong to be abused. I thought it was because I was a bad kid. (I wasn't.) . . . I seem to always mess up and I didn't want God to be mad at me.

He said, "There is nothing you could do that could ever change the way God feels about you." . . . I said, "I wish God loved me like the people in the Bible." He said, "He does!" . . . I can't tell you my feelings through all this. I wish I could download it and send it to everyone. Like every particle that is making up who you are is bursting with LOVE & Bliss. I said, "I just want to be with God, I just want to be with You!" He said, "You will!"

At this time, I turned around. . . . His eyes were wide with excitement and overflowing with LOVE and JOY. . . . There is no living person to ever exist that could match the BEAUTY of Jesus Christ. . . . He embraced me and held me so close. . . . I said to Jesus, "You mean I don't have to go to sleep forever?" He laughed and said, "No." Jesus told me I was going to live forever and I would never die. He said this place was my HOME.[1]

There is nothing you could ever do that would change the way God feels about you. He delighted in his wonderful creation when he made you, and you delight his heart now.

As King David sings about in Psalm 139, you are fearfully and wonderfully made! And when you see yourself the way God sees you, created by him with unique value and purpose, it will encourage you to live out the dream God has for you as you follow his leadership in your life. God made you unique for a reason. He sees your full potential, and he desires for you to experience all he created you to be.

He loves and accepts you just as you are. He calls you beautiful, special, and his beloved child. This is the truth about you, nothing less. Soak in how God feels about you today, and let his love fill you up with joy in his presence.

> **Prayer:** *Dear Father, thank you for loving, accepting, and delighting in me. Help me to see myself the way you do, as your unique and wonderful creation.*

4

If we don't love people we can see, how can we love God, whom we cannot see? And he has given us this command: Those who love God must also love their fellow believers.

1 John 4:20–21

STEVE SJOGREN WAS THE PASTOR of a large church doing lots of good serving Cincinnati in thousands of ways. No doubt that was part of God's purpose for Steve, but Steve's brush with death reminded him of God's priorities for us. Steve humbly recalls:

God got me good. I was hovering over the operating table as close to the ceiling as I could get without actually leaving the room. . . . I knew intuitively that God was the one who was addressing me. It was like the voice of a hundred friends talking in harmonious unison. . . . We did not communicate just with words, but also with memories and images.

God let me know how much He valued me. It's almost impossible to describe the perfect sense of acceptance that surrounded me, yet even in the midst of this very personal embrace, part of me knew that not everything in my life had matched what God had intended for me. . . .

The doctors were in emergency mode and God was calmly quizzing me. "Do you know the names of your children's friends?" He asked. This was not a daydream. God wanted to know the answer, but I couldn't list a single one! I was caught dead to rights. The realization struck me like a bolt of lightning. I hadn't taken the time to get to know my children's best friends and long-term buddies, let alone the new classmate Laura had brought over a few weeks earlier. My oversight was embarrassing and inexcusable. These friends often visited our house. They were always welcome, but I was anything but hospitable. When they came, I was usually fixated on one project or another. Many times, I just wasn't there. My job was important, after all.

While working hard is good, being totally immersed in work to the point of excluding family members is a fatal error. I found out the hard way. In my case, this error was not terminal, but it was a close call. Since that day in the operating room, I have gone to my children—all three of them—and asked each one to forgive me. I told them that I was not an example of a good father, much less a good pastor.[1]

Even though we may know that loving God and loving people is what is most important to God, they are often difficult to prioritize over all the to-do lists screaming for our attention. The distractions the internet can bring, along with the temptation to constantly be multitasking, can make this even harder for us. Yet when we focus on these two things God prioritizes most, God's will and ways will naturally work in our lives.

God knows your name and the number of hairs on your head, and he cares about developing the unique, wonderful person he made you to be. He wants you to view the people in your life the same—take interest in them, spend time enjoying them as God's beloved, truly value things that are important to them, and care about what brings them joy. This delights the heart of God, and will bring joy into your life as well.

Prioritizing people is actually one of the most productive ways to spend your time, and relationships are at the center of God's heart. As you do life with your children, spouse, family, and friends today, be proactive about taking the time to value them as God does, and see the blessings that will flow.

> **Prayer:** *Dear God, I am so grateful you know me so intimately and love me so much. Help me prioritize the people in my life and show them the same love, making time to fully enjoy being with them.*

5

But you are a chosen people, a royal priesthood, a holy nation, God's special possession, that you may declare the praises of him who called you out of darkness into his wonderful light.

1 Peter 2:9

Jamie from Texas gained insight into what this verse means when complications arose during her surgery.

My first memory of being in ICU was to awaken to seeing a team of doctors around my bed. They told me I was bleeding internally and the doctors were trying to stop it without having to do surgery. . . . The last thing the doctors told my family was that it's up to him now while pointing to heaven. . . . This is how I remember what happened.

I felt like I was in the presence of someone that I had always known. My spirit felt it more than my mind did. I said, "You're Jesus, aren't you?" He gave me that smile that only Jesus can give and I knew the answer without him having to say anything. We walked and talked for a while beside the River of Life.

One of the many things I loved there was that Jesus and I did not verbally speak to each other. He knew and answered my thoughts and I didn't need to open my mouth. . . . I looked off into the distance behind me. I could see a line of people walking across a bridge. When they were on my side of the bridge, they looked dull. Once on the other side, they were wearing white garments and looked bright.

I looked at Jesus and asked if that was the way to Heaven. He smiled and said, "Yes." I then asked, "Can I go there right now?" Jesus said, "Yes, you may go. God is ready for you anytime you are ready to go home." I said, "Yes, I'm ready." At that point I said, "I want my husband to go with me." Jesus smiled that forever patient loving smile of his and said, "God is not ready for him yet, he can't go with you." So I looked at Jesus and said, "I don't want to go to heaven without my husband. . . ."

. . . Jesus took both my hands, turning my palms upward. While holding my hands he said, "I want you to remember something. You are of a royal lineage. You are a child of God. The Most High God. You live in the world, but are not of the world. Your rightful place is in heaven with the Father." I said, "Yes, I understand." The whole while he was telling me this, I felt like I was the most precious, most loved, most beloved person in existence.

Next, I asked, "Just what is your relationship to me?" Jesus said, "I am your brother." I said, "I know that's what the Bible says, so it's true then?" Jesus said, "Yes, I am your brother. We have the same blood running through our veins. I will never leave you or forsake you. I will always be there for you. Never ever forget who you are."[1]

It is a mystery how God, in his infinite mercy and love, united himself to humanity through Jesus. Jesus is both Creator God (John 1:3) and our brother (Heb. 2:10). He humbled himself to adopt us and to bring us back into his family. He is the King, and you are his beloved royal daughter or son. When you begin to see yourself this way, it can help you to live with confidence and boldness for Christ, as a member of his royal family.

Hebrews 2:10–11 says, "In bringing many sons and daughters to glory, it was fitting that God, for whom and through whom everything exists, should make the pioneer of their salvation perfect through what he suffered. Both the one who makes people holy and those who are made holy are of the same family. So Jesus is not ashamed to call them brothers and sisters."

Jesus brought you out of darkness and into the light and calls himself your brother! Today, live as a child of the King and identify boldly with the royal family to which you belong.

> **Prayer:** *Dear Heavenly Father, thank you for adopting me into your royal family. Help me to live confidently in your will as a child of the Most High King.*

6

I am with you always, to the very end of the age.

Matthew 28:20

AT AGE FIVE, Margret was misdiagnosed with scarlet fever. In reality, her appendix had ruptured, and the infection took her to the edge of death. One night, says Margret,

This marvelous feeling of peace came over me. I was basking in that because it was so beautiful, when suddenly I became aware that someone was holding my right hand. I looked up and my eyes were traveling over a white gown. I came to the head of this beautiful woman. . . .

She walked along with me holding my hand. . . . I became aware of a fragrance in the air that was becoming stronger and stronger. It was of flowers, and they just seemed to permeate my whole body. And when I took notice of what was around me besides her, I realized that the path was banked with flowers way over our heads. These flowers were close together the way a Colonial bouquet would be, and they were massive. I was just so overwhelmed by this fragrance that I said to her like a little kid, which I was, "Are these flowers real?"

She smiled and looked down at me and said, "Yes they are." I could see her chuckling, trying to hold back a laugh.

After this beautiful woman told her she must go back, it took Margret a year to recover. Decades later, in her sixties, she decided to paint the beautiful arbor pathway of Heaven. While painting it, Margret had to see her doctor. Her doctor mentioned near-death experiences, and she told him she was painting hers. He asked for a reproduction of it, and the doctor ended up hanging Margret's painting among ten other pictures in his office.

Several weeks later, a new patient named Mary Olivia came into the doctor's office. As a single mom facing a terminal illness with three children, she needed a second opinion. When Mary Olivia saw the painting in the doctor's office, she just stood and stared for several minutes before exclaiming to the doctor,

"I know where this is."

He said, "You know what that's a picture of?"

"Of course I do. I walked along that path when I was five years old and almost died."

Mary Olivia then recalled how THE MAN (capitalized at her request) said he would always be with her as they walked beneath the arbor's beautiful flowers, and this gave her comfort as she was there at the doctor.

After learning of Mary Olivia's story, Margret feels God led her to paint that picture because Mary Olivia needed to be reminded of Jesus's words, "I'm always with you" (Matt. 28:20).[1]

It is amazing when we realize how personal Jesus is with each of us, even to the point of orchestrating moments in time to meet a need he knows we will have in the future. Being aware of his presence enables us to live each day with a calm assurance that there is nothing we will face without Jesus by our side.

As a child feels safe with a loving parent beside her, you can feel that same security with your Heavenly Father promising to always be with you. Let this truth reassure you today. Jesus wants to help you live with the courage and confidence you need to face the challenges ahead. You are never alone, and that is a promise!

Prayer: *Heavenly Father, I am so grateful that you are always with me, and I can trust in you to walk alongside me through every challenge and every joy I may face in life. Help me to lean on you, and let your love guide me as I live each day for your purposes.*

7

Jesus spoke to the people once more and said, "I am the light of the world. If you follow me, you won't have to walk in darkness, because you will have the light that leads to life."

John 8:12 NLT

For you are the fountain of life, the light by which we see.

Psalm 36:9 NLT

BRAD BARROWS HAD BEEN BLIND since birth and had an NDE at age eight. He recalls "seeing" his lifeless body on the bed, "seeing" light and colors, but then being pulled upward into a tunnel:

When I actually got into the tunnel, I do remember that one thing that puzzled me was the lack of any color. . . . There was no color whatsoever. It was as black as I can understand blackness to be. But coming out into [a] large field, the closest I could tell you about color was that the brightness and brilliance of that whole area was absolutely indescribable.

I could not distinguish fine shades of color, for some reason. It's possible that I could have, but I had no vocabulary to describe it. . . . My concept of colors, my perception of colors, still remained absolutely beyond my reach. . . . I felt as if I might be entering another realm altogether, an unexplained dimension that I had very little understanding of. . . .

When I noticed that I was walking up this field, it seemed as if I was so exhilarated and so unbelievably renewed that I didn't want to leave. I wanted to stay forever where I was. . . . It was so unbelievably peaceful that there [is] no way that I could describe the peace and the tranquility and the calm. . . .

There was tremendous light up there. It seemed to come from every direction. . . . It was all around and everywhere that I happened to be looking. . . . It seemed like everything, even the grass I had been stepping on seemed to soak in that light.

Brad also became aware of thousands of voices singing:

I remember thinking that the voices seemed to be singing in a language I had never understood or maybe many, many languages. The music I had heard was nothing like anything I have ever experienced. . . .

Within a very short amount of time . . . I came to a large stone structure. I could tell that it was stone without even touching it. . . . They were almost like gem stones. They seemed to literally shine with their own particular light. Yet the light itself was actually penetrating right through the stones.[1]

It is awe-inspiring to think of how a blind person must feel as they see for the first time the glorious sights and wonders of Heaven! Revelation 21:23 tells us, "The city [of God] does not need the sun or the moon to shine on it, for the glory of God gives it light, and the Lamb is its lamp."

At the same time, just as Jesus lights up heaven with his glory, Jesus is also the spiritual light of the world you live in today! He wants to lead you in a life that satisfies your deepest longings. As you follow Jesus, he will light the way before you step by step. His light will illuminate the purpose he desires uniquely for you, a purpose that only you can fulfill.

Today, allow his light and love to guide you, and you will experience more of Heaven on earth as you face the challenges each day brings. His light will dispel the spiritual darkness, and you'll see the blessings he has before you in renewed ways.

Prayer: *Jesus, thank you for guiding me in your light and love so that I never have to be in the darkness. Help me to follow you fully and walk in your light today and always.*

8

Love must be sincere. Hate what is evil; cling to what is good. Be devoted to one another in love. Honor one another above yourselves. Never be lacking in zeal, but keep your spiritual fervor, serving the Lord.

Romans 12:9–11

THOSE WHO COME BACK from a glimpse of Heaven often adopt different priorities. They realize the external emphasis we put on life is trivial, whereas the spiritual aspects of life matter supremely. One man shares:

> We are what we think. I find trivial thoughts distracting, I rarely watch TV and then only if it stimulates good thoughts. I listen to different music now. . . . My near-death experience has changed me, I desire righteousness and I abhor evil. I'm actually quite thankful for my accident, even though it has changed my physical abilities adversely, but at the same time my spiritual abilities have blossomed enormously! Ever since I woke up from my coma, I've had an attitude of peaceful hopefulness. I believe the reason why I still live, one of the reasons I came back to this earth to live, is because I'm supposed to testify that the spirit world is real and beautiful, and that Jesus is who he says he is.[1]

Another person noticed the wonders of a life with the complete absence of evil:

> Part of the joy I was experiencing was not only the presence of everything wonderful but the absence of everything terrible. There was no strife, no competition, no sarcasm, no betrayal, no deception, no lies, no murders, no unfaithfulness, no disloyalty, nothing contrary to the light and life and love. . . . The absence of sin was something you could feel. There was no shame, because there was nothing to be ashamed of. There was no sadness, because there

was nothing to be sad about. There was no need to hide, because there was nothing to hide from. It was all out in the open.[2]

Imagine a place where all evil is gone and only good prevails! There is a real place like that—Heaven will be that place, and we will be able to live in that goodness all the days of our lives for an eternity. Imagine only peace, love, joy, kindness, and gentleness inhabiting space in our lives and relationships. How amazing it will be with no negativity, unkindness, hatred, or self-centeredness ever to endure again!

This sounds like the most wonderful place to be, yet far from what we experience in our broken world. Even so, God wants to help us overcome the evils on earth and experience more of his goodness in our lives today. With God's power, we can fight evil with good.

The loving-kindness and goodness of God can overcome hate and destruction, one willing heart at a time. As a believer, you have the Source living within you, the Holy Spirit, to demonstrate the character of God to those around you. The good news is that when you remain connected to his Spirit, you will naturally shine his love out in the world. Where God's love radiates, evil loses its power.

Commit today to conquering evil with God's goodness and love. This may be as you honor others above yourself, encourage people the way you want to be encouraged, and love even those who don't love you, by serving them as an act of love for God. The ripple effects of your kindness and love can be a powerful force in bringing Heaven to earth.

Prayer: *Dear God, thank you that in Heaven, all evil is gone and only goodness remains. Help me to fight the evil in our world with your love, knowing that love will win in the end.*

9

Our present sufferings are not worth comparing with the glory that will be revealed in us. . . . We know that the whole creation has been groaning as in the pains of childbirth right up to the present time.

Romans 8:18, 22

ARV BESTEMAN, a retired bank president, had surgery at the University of Michigan Medical Center to remove a rare pancreatic tumor called an insulinoma. It was after visiting hours, and his family had gone home for the night. Marv recalls:

I was alone and racked with pain and more than a little bit grumpy as I tossed and turned; more than anything, I just wanted to sleep and escape the misery and discomfort for just a little while. I had no idea I was about to get an escape beyond my wildest dreams. . . .

Suddenly, two men I had never seen before in my life walked into my hospital room. Don't ask me how I knew, but immediately I had a sense that these men were angels. I wasn't the least bit anxious, either. Once they had detached me from my tangle of tubes [which Marv later reflected was unnecessary, but probably for his benefit as a high-control banker], the angels gathered me in their arms and we began to ascend, on a quick journey that felt light and smooth through the bluest of blue skies. I was deposited on solid ground, in front of a monumental gate. And no, I don't remember it as being "pearly." . . .

I saw color-bursts that lit up the sky, way beyond the northern lights I had seen once on a trip to Alaska. Simply glorious. . . . The music I heard was incomparable to anything I had ever heard before. There was a choir of a million people. . . . It was the most lush and beautiful music I had ever heard. And do you know that every single day since my experience I have heard a few snatches of that music? I am so blessed to remember that heavenly sound. . . .

My [old] geezer body felt young and strong and fantastic. The aches and pains and limitations of age were just gone. I felt like a teenager again, only better.[1]

Remember what it was like to have endless energy as a child? Recall the strength and stamina of those teen years? In the life to come, not only will we be free of the pains and worries of this earthly body, we will feel young again! When the little children flocked to Jesus, he said, "The kingdom of God belongs to such as these" (Luke 18:16). It is comforting to know that the sufferings of this life are just "birth pains" preparing us for a time where the innocence, wonder, and excitement we felt as children are reborn in us.

Sometimes it might be hard to imagine feeling energetic and strong again, when you must cope with so much hardship here on earth. Your current sufferings matter to God, and he eternally rewards those who endure by faith. He is full of compassion and cares about what you are going through. God promises you that your sufferings in this life will be nothing compared to the vibrant, pain-free life you will experience forever in Heaven! You can stand on this promise and let it empower you to live with purpose each day.

Jesus wants to enter into your suffering with you to carry you through it. He can give you joy even through the difficulties of life. Lean on him today in your trials and hardships, and remember to pray for those experiencing the same. Hold on to the hope of Heaven where all will be restored!

Prayer: *Heavenly Father, I want to focus on the promise of heaven even during the hardships and trials on earth. Thank you for entering into my suffering and rewarding me as I persevere through it, knowing it counts eternally.*

10

Use your worldly resources to benefit others and make friends. Then, when your possessions are gone, they will welcome you to an eternal home.

Luke 16:9 NLT

DON PIPER WAS COMING BACK from a pastors' conference when an 18-wheeler lost control on a rainy bridge and hit him head-on. EMS pronounced him dead, and for ninety minutes Don's body lay trapped in the car while EMS waited for the Jaws of Life to cut him out of the wreckage.

Simultaneous with my last recollection of seeing the bridge and the rain, a light enveloped me, with a brilliance beyond earthly comprehension or description. Only that. In my next moment of awareness, I was standing in heaven.

Joy pulsated through me as I looked around, and at that moment I became aware of a large crowd of people. They stood in front of a brilliant, ornate gate. . . . As the crowd rushed toward me, I didn't see Jesus, but I did see people I had known. As they surged toward me, I knew instantly that all of them had died during my lifetime.

Their presence seemed absolutely natural. They rushed toward me, and every person was smiling, shouting, and praising God. Although no one said so, intuitively I knew they were my celestial welcoming committee. It was as if they had all gathered just outside heaven's gate, waiting for me.

The first person I recognized was Joe Kulbeth, my grandfather. He looked exactly as I remembered him, with his shock of white hair and what I called a big banana nose. He stopped momentarily and stood in front of me. A grin covered his face. I may have called his name, but I'm not sure. "Donnie!" (That's what my grandfather always called me.) His eyes lit up, and he held out his arms as he took the last steps toward me. He embraced me, holding me tightly. He was once again the robust, strong grandfather I had remembered as a child. . . .

The crowd surrounded me. Some hugged me and a few kissed my cheek, while others pumped my hand. Never had I felt more loved. One person in that greeting committee was Mike Wood, my childhood friend. Mike was special because he invited me to Sunday school and was influential in my becoming a Christian. Mike was the most devoted young Christian I knew. He was also a popular kid and had lettered four years in football, basketball, and track. . . .

When he was nineteen, Mike was killed in a car wreck. It broke my heart. . . . Now I saw Mike in heaven. As he slipped his arm around my shoulder, my pain and grief vanished. Never had I seen Mike smile so brightly. Everything felt blissful. Perfect.[1]

How we treat others and invest in them—family, friends, neighbors, coworkers—is actually an eternal investment we make that will reap infinite rewards. This includes a tribe of friends that Jesus says will welcome you into Heaven!

You may feel like much of your time spent serving others goes unnoticed, or you may feel exhausted as you care for people who need you in ways only you can meet. God sees all of this, and he cares. He notices the acts of kindness and encouragement you give and the time and energy you sacrifice to develop others.

Remember, the friendships made here on earth will continue on in even greater depth of enjoyment in Heaven! You'll experience the ripple effect of the impact you've made on people's lives, resulting in richer relationships to come. Focus on this as you invest in the lives God has given you today, and let it motivate you to continue to love and serve others as he leads.

Prayer: *Jesus, thank you for the life-giving relationships you have blessed me with, and for the opportunities you have given me to serve others.*

11

Jesus replied: "'Love the Lord your God with all your heart and with all your soul and with all your mind.' This is the first and greatest commandment. And the second is like it: 'Love your neighbor as yourself.' All the Law and the Prophets hang on these two commandments."

Matthew 22:37–40

WHAT IS YOUR PURPOSE? How do you know what God has you uniquely here to do? Often we make it complicated, but it is really quite simple at the core. In a personal interview, Dr. Mary Neal talks about gaining insight into God's plan for our lives during her NDE:

I find so many people are either living in regret from yesterday, or they're focused on tomorrow, [and] they forget about right now, right here, this very moment.

When I was on the threshold of this dome structure [she described like a Heavenly city], I had this absolute sense of understanding, of getting it, of being able to understand the divine nature of everything. Or, not so much the divine nature, but understanding the divine order of everything and how everything is interconnected. . . .

I also had this—for me—very profound understanding of how it can be true that God actually knows each and every one of us—all the billions of us on the planet—loves each and every one of us as though we are the only ones, and has a plan for each and every one of our lives that's one of hope. And that understanding alone creates even more pressure, every moment of every day, to constantly be questioning and constantly be asking yourself, "Okay, in this very moment, am I following the plan that God would have for me?" Because God's plans for us are always greater than we can imagine. . . .

We need to be about God's business every moment of every day. One of the things that changed for me very dramatically is—and

I believe it can change anyone's life—is that, if you accept that there's life after death and then, even more so, if you accept the rest of God's promises . . . it changes the way you see today. Because, all of a sudden, every day matters, every moment matters, every choice, every decision, it matters.

We think about our lifetime as so long, but in reality, it's a blink of time. And the reality is that we are here for a reason. We are here to learn and grow and change and help others do the same. And we don't have much time to do it.

There is no doubt that the only thing that truly matters is loving God and being a window through which God's light can shine through this world, and loving each other.[1]

God has us uniquely here for a purpose—and love is what it is about, no matter what else we accomplish. As Jesus says in Matthew 22, the two most important commandments—love God and love people—sum up all the rest. Loving God, and letting his love shine through us to love others, is central to our purpose.

As you seek and respond to God's guidance in the decisions you make, you align yourself to the plan he has for your life. God cares about who he created you to become. It brings him delight when he sees you living out your full potential and participating in his work in the world! As Paul wrote in Ephesians 2:10, "He creates each of us by Christ Jesus to join him in the work he does, the good work he has gotten ready for us to do, work we had better be doing" (MSG).

Today, be aware of the people you pass and the situations God puts before you. You'll see how he will lead you into meaningful and loving interaction with them, participating in his grand purpose and plan to make a difference in the world through you.

> **Prayer:** *Lord, help me each day to fulfill what you have placed me on earth to do. May my life be characterized by love for you and love for others wherever I live and through whatever I do.*

12

He who was seated on the throne said, "I am making everything new!"

Revelation 21:5

RICHARD DIED in a horrible car accident. The medics said he was already dead when they found him, but he revived to describe the beauty of Heaven and the new life found within.

I was walking through a garden that stretched for as far as I could see in either direction. And I saw great groups of people.

On either side of the pathway was the richest turf-green grass I had ever seen. And it was moving with life and energy. . . . There were flowers of every imaginable size and color along the path. There were banks and banks of flowers. . . . The air was filled with their aroma, and they were all humming. I asked if I could pick one to smell, and I was told that I could. It was wonderful. When I put the flower down, it was immediately replanted and growing again. Again, there's no death in heaven. . . .

As I walked along the golden pathway, I noticed the sky. It was rosette-pinkish in color, but it was also a crystal-clear blue. And there were clouds in the sky—clouds of glory. When I looked more closely at them I saw that the "clouds" were actually thousands of angels. . . .

The beautifully manicured park was filled with huge, striking trees. They had to be at least two thousand feet tall. And there were many different varieties. Some I knew; others, I had no idea what species they were. But they were tall and strong, with no dead branches or limbs. There was not even a dead leaf. . . .

There was a continual sound of chimes coming from the leaves [of one tree] as they brushed against one another in the gentle breeze—the beautiful sound of crystal. When I touched them, there was a glow as the sound emanated from them.

But there was more. Each leaf, each limb—the entire tree—gave off a tremendous glow with all the colors that were in the glory cloud. The tree glowed with sound and light. It was also aflame with glory. . . .

I went up to what I thought was a walnut tree, and I was told to take and eat. The fruit was pear shaped and copper colored. When I picked it, another fruit instantly grew in its place. When I touched the fruit to my lips, it evaporated and melted into the most delicious thing I had ever tasted. It was like honey, peach juice, and pear juice. It was sweet but not sugary. . . . It was a wonderful experience, and I can almost still taste that delicious juice after all this time.

There were also trees whose leaves were shaped like hearts and gave off a beautiful aroma. I was told to take a leaf and smell it, and so I did. Then, a voice told me that it would give me strength to carry on. The moment I smelled the beautiful fragrance, I was strengthened.[1]

Imagine what it will be like to experience this kind of beauty and splendor, with new and amazing surroundings, and life-giving strength to explore it all! One day you will, and what a glorious day that will be!

Everything you know on earth will be made new, in its most beautiful and magnificent form. The frustrations of disorder and entropy that constantly plague our world will be gone. In fact, the beauty you already experience on earth—majestic mountains, turquoise seas, palm tree–lined beaches, magnificent glaciers and canyons—all reflect the splendor and glory of God that you will one day experience in perfection.

Today, as you see the world around you, imagine how all of creation will be in new and perfect form in Heaven, beyond your wildest dreams. Let this bring you expectant hope for your life even now.

Prayer: *Lord, I praise you that the heavens declare your glory, and one day I will experience it all with you. How amazing it will be to enjoy your creation in perfect form for eternity! I worship you today as the One who is making all things new.*

13

The earnest prayer of a righteous person has great power and produces wonderful results.

James 5:16 NLT

WHILE SCUBA DIVING off an island in the Indian Ocean, twenty-four-year-old Ian McCormack was stung multiple times by a school of box jellyfish—and one sting is deadly! In the ambulance, Ian's life began to vividly replay before his eyes. "People say just before they die, their life flashes before them." Ian recalls:

> My thoughts were racing. "I'm too young to die, why did I go diving?" . . . I lay there wondering what would happen if I died? Is there anything after I die? Where would I go if I died?
>
> Then I saw a clear vision of my mother. It was as though she was speaking out those words she had spoken so long ago: "Ian, no matter how far from God you are, no matter what you've done wrong, if you cry out to God from your heart, he will hear you and he will forgive you."
>
> In my heart I was thinking, "Do I believe there is a God? Am I going to pray?" I'd almost become a devout atheist. I didn't believe anybody.[1]

At the same time, thousands of miles away in New Zealand, Ian's mother awoke from a dream with an urgent sense that her son was in trouble. She began praying for him with all her might. Back in the ocean, Ian began to pray as well.

> I didn't know what to pray or whom to pray to. Which god should I pray to? Buddha? Kali? Shiva? There are thousands of them. Yet I didn't see Buddha or Krishna or some other god or man standing there, I saw my mother—and my mother followed Jesus Christ. I wondered what I should pray. . . . "God, I ask you to forgive my sins, but I've done so many wrong things . . . but please forgive me of my sins."[2]

As he was praying, Ian breathed his last breath. At first, he found himself in a very dark place.

> Then a brilliant light shone upon me and literally drew me out of the darkness. . . . It looked unspeakably bright, as if it was the centre of the universe, the source of all light and power. It was more brilliant than the sun, more radiant than any diamond, brighter than a laser beam. Yet you could look right into it. . . .
>
> I found myself beginning to weep uncontrollably as the love became stronger and stronger. It was so clean and pure, no strings attached. . . .
>
> As I stepped into the light it was as if I'd come inside veils of suspended shimmering lights, like suspended stars or diamonds giving off the most amazing radiance. And as I walked through the light it continued to heal the deepest part of me. . . .
>
> As I lifted my eyes up, I could see the chest of a man with his arms outstretched as if to welcome me.[3]

Stories like these remind us how powerful our prayers really are! The seeds of faith we plant, and our faithful prayers for our loved ones to know Jesus, will not return void. Even though sometimes we may feel like our prayers are not being heard, *they are*, and God will move through them at the right time.

Our heartfelt prayers for wayward children, prayers for our spouse, friends, and coworkers—God hears all of these, and his timing is perfect. We can trust that he is working through our perseverance and persistence, and no prayer goes unanswered. It may take years. It may even take until someone's dying moment. But God will act when the time is right.

Keep being persistent; God never tires of hearing your requests! As you pray today, look forward with expectancy to the ways he will answer, and thank him in advance for his faithfulness.

Prayer: *Heavenly Father, thank you that you hear my requests. I will be persistent, trusting in your perfect timing.*

14

Even before he made the world, God loved us and chose us in Christ to be holy and without fault in his eyes.

Ephesians 1:4 NLT

CARLA HAD BEEN BLIND FROM BIRTH, but she finally saw the truth during her life review. Carla clinically died during surgery, left her body, and accurately described the operating room: "The operating table was in the center of the room . . . the screen for the telemetry was on the ceiling." This confirmed to the hospital staff that she truly experienced something real. During her life review, she saw the truth about the bullying she endured:

Interviewer: Were you able to see details of people that you had never been able to see?

Carla: Oh, yeah. But I saw, you know, myself [and] how I was dealing with people and the exact things that I had said, you know, to these people throughout each experience.

Interviewer: Is there anything that you can describe visually that you couldn't have seen before this? Did any particular event stand out?

Carla: Well, a lot of the events were from my childhood and events from school. . . . I grew up tall and grew physically before my age, and so the kids who were partially sighted used to call me "big barn." And I think that through this, as I could see myself on the playground or swimming or doing whatever it was I was doing, that I was not the way they depicted me. That in actuality, some

	of the kids who made fun of me were bigger and fatter than me, you know, and I could see this.
Interviewer:	Did that surprise you?
Carla:	Yeah, it really did. It gave me the feeling then that, "hey, you're not so bad." You know how when you have kind of an emotional realization. And so it doesn't sound like a big deal [but] it really was to me. . . . I thought that I looked like a really graceful person. Like "a lady."[1]

Sometimes you may find yourself forming your identity from what others say you are, or perhaps from the opinions you perceive others have of you. Regardless, God says that you are his special possession, his beautiful, wonderful creation! He makes no mistakes, and you can trust him, confident in your worth and importance in the world.

You are a child of the King! When you realize this, it can completely change the way you live your life and the way you view yourself in the world. You are a treasure with a unique contribution to make while you are here on earth. God is the only one you need to please, and he sees you as the beautiful masterpiece he created you to be, full of potential and immeasurable value.

He loves you just as you are. Don't waste any more time feeling negatively about yourself from what others have said or done to you. If you have heard lies in the past about your worth or importance, start today by resisting those lies and replacing them with the truth about you. God wants you to feel as loved and treasured as you truly are, so you can begin living that way!

Prayer: *Dear God, thank you for loving me so much and for seeing me as I truly am, your beautiful creation. Help me to find my identity in you alone.*

15

Jesus straightened up and asked her, "Woman, where are they? Has no one condemned you?" "No one, sir," she said. "Then neither do I condemn you," Jesus declared.

John 8:10–11

ONE OF THE GREATEST INDICATIONS that the God NDErs describe is the God of the Jewish/Christian Scriptures is how they depict their life review in his presence. Despite vividly seeing all their deeds, good and bad, and all the relational ripple effects of both, they do not experience a God who desires to condemn. They experience an extraordinary compassion coming from this God of light and love.

Yet if you search the gods of the world's religions, how many of them claim to uphold both justice and righteousness, record our every thought and deed, and still hold out forgiveness and compassion because of a desire for loving relationship? Only the God of the Bible.

A woman experienced all this during her life review in Jesus's presence:

Everything I ever thought, did, said, hated, helped, did not help, should have helped was shown in front of me, the crowd of hundreds, and everyone like [in] a movie. How mean I'd been to people, how I could have helped them, how mean I was (unintentionally also) to animals! Yes! Even the animals had had feelings. It was horrible. I fell on my face in shame. I saw how my acting, or not acting, rippled in effect towards other people and their lives. It wasn't until then that I understood how each little decision or choice affects the world. The sense of letting my Savior down was too real. Strangely, even during this horror, I felt a compassion, an acceptance of my limitations by Jesus and the crowd of others.[1]

The fact that people experience compassion instead of judgment makes some NDE researchers conclude this can't be the God of the Bible, yet they do not really understand what the Bible teaches. When a woman caught in adultery was brought to Jesus by the religious leaders who wanted to condemn her and stone her to death, Jesus said to them, "Let any one of you who is without sin be the first to throw a stone at her." They all dropped their rocks and left. "Has no one condemned you?" Jesus asked her. "No one, sir," she said. "Then neither do I condemn you," Jesus declared. "Go now and leave your life of sin" (see John 8:2–11).

God loves us so much. He doesn't stand ready to condemn us but reaches out with mercy to every one of his children, no matter what wrongs we have done. In his justice and mercy, he paid the penalty to set us free and redeem us through what Jesus did on the cross. Jesus said this is what he came to do: "For God so loved the world that he gave his one and only Son, that whoever believes in him shall not perish but have eternal life. For God did not send his Son into the world to condemn the world, but to save the world through him" (John 3:16–17).

If you have told God, *I want what Jesus did to count for me—I need your forgiveness and leadership in my life*, then you don't need to fear judgment or condemnation from anyone. God declares you right in his sight forever!

Do you live in that freedom? Don't let anything keep you from reaching out to Jesus, for he has set you free. And don't let fear of what others think, or their judgment of you, have any place in your life. Jesus has set you free from all condemnation, so that you might follow him and experience the abundant life only he can give.

> **Prayer:** *Lord Jesus, thank you that you did not come to condemn the world but to save those who believe in you. Help me to live free in you, experiencing your mercy and grace each day as I follow your will for my life.*

16

Jesus said, "Let the little children come to me, and do not hinder them, for the kingdom of heaven belongs to such as these."

Matthew 19:14

MEGAN WAS SIX YEARS OLD when she experienced the wonders of heaven during a sleep apnea episode. What impacted her then, and what sticks with her even today, was her encounter with the angels and how important they made her feel.

I was asleep when two angels woke me up and took me to Heaven. . . . After a while, they said we had some time, and we could do anything I would like to do. I said I'd like to play the board game *Candy Land*, since my friends didn't like playing it any more.

The angels materialized the game, and asked me to teach them how to play. I did, and as they were learning, they were laughing with deep joy, as if there was nothing better ever than playing that game with me! I was feeling such joy in that moment that when I was told I must go back, I resisted.

We were sitting on what looked like a cloud bank of orange-ish pink, fluffy, soft stuff. One angel waved his hand over the clouds, clearing a space. I looked down at my elementary school from above. The sun was just coming up and the lights were just starting to come on in the school. He said if I didn't return, my friends and teachers at school would miss me and be sad. (I still did not want to go back!) Then he waved his hand again, and I was up in the corner of the kitchen ceiling, looking down at my mom getting breakfast ready. The angel said if I didn't go back, my mom would be really sad. So at that point, I agreed to go. The angels reassured me they would always be with me to help me.

One of the greatest gifts I received from my time with the two angels was experiencing their joy in being with me, like there was nothing better in the universe than that. . . . I feel this is one of the greatest gifts we can give to one another too. It is joy-gratitude and appreciation inherent in being with someone. This greatly influenced how I raised my daughter—to impart that sense that I would love nothing more than to be with her whenever she and I were together.[1]

Children are precious in God's sight! Jesus demonstrated his delight in them during his life on earth. Even amid all the demands of his ministry, he still made time to gather the little ones on his lap and pay attention to them. Jesus was fully aware of the short time he had before his earthly life would end, and he had much business to do for the kingdom, yet he still prioritized the children when they were in his presence.

It brings God joy when you take time for his little ones. Focus on delighting in just being with them—they are God's precious masterpieces! Enjoy loving them with God's love. God notices everything you do—the diaper changing, lullabies, bedtime stories, hugs and kisses, caregiving, mentoring, lunches packed, carpooling, homework help, recitals, ballgames, late-night talks—these all matter! As Jesus promises in Matthew 10:42, "And if anyone gives even a cup of cold water to one of these little ones . . . I tell you, that person will certainly not lose their reward."

All your time spent loving and valuing God's children through all of their ages and stages is extremely important to him, and he will reward you for the ways you bless their lives. So today, enjoy investing in and loving the children in your life—yours, or even a friend's. When you are with them, be fully present and take delight in the treasures they are, just as Jesus did.

Prayer: *Dear Father, help me to value the precious children in my life, giving them my full attention and time when I am with them. Let them see how much you adore them through my love and delight in them.*

17

Praise be to the God and Father of our Lord Jesus Christ,
the Father of compassion and the God of all comfort. . . .
For just as we share abundantly in the sufferings of Christ,
so also our comfort abounds through Christ.

2 Corinthians 1:3, 5

MARCY WAS A CHRISTIAN who had wandered far from the Lord in despair due to ongoing marital struggles. During her NDE, she experienced the most extravagant comfort from God himself.

I was being pulled through a tunnel with the light getting brighter and brighter. After a while, I was suddenly standing in front of this beautiful wrought iron Victorian gate, covered with the largest and most brilliant colored flowers I had ever seen. . . .

Just before I entered, a voice in my mind spoke to me. I turned to look to my left and there stood Jesus Christ. I could see his nail prints in his hands and feet. But they were not in his hands; they were more in his wrist area and angled out as though they were torn from his weight. There was no verbal speaking, just mental telepathy. I ran to him and wrapped my arms around his feet, kissing his feet, and telling him how much I loved him . . . his arms came down and he held my head close to him as I cried hard. . . .

I could tell that I was standing at the base of a huge stairway (I called it a huge throne) with the most brilliant light shining down from it. It was God. Jesus was standing on the right hand of God at the base of his throne. I began talking to God, telling him how much I loved him and Jesus. . . . At that point, I could tell that Jesus was communicating with God . . . telling God how much I loved him and believed that he died for my sins. God then spoke mentally to me and told me how much he loved me. (Jesus was the mediator between God and me). . . . God spoke mentally to me and told me to go back; your time has not yet come. I pleaded with him and fell to my knees, begging him not to send me back. No thought of the world was inside of me; it was all heavenly minded.

I was crying and begging so loud[ly] that I suddenly felt God's arms come down (there were no arms but I felt them), and he lifted me off my feet and cradled me as a mother cradles her baby against her breast. He rocked me and held me in his arms. He gently placed me back to my feet and then told me that I had to go back, because I have children that were going to be born to me, and I needed to go back and receive his gift of children. (The doctors told me I could not have children before I died.)

The second that God told me he was giving me children, I immediately became earthly minded and began my trip back through this vast area, until I was again hovering over my body in bed. I felt my feet enter through my fleshly head and lower itself into my lifeless body. When I opened my eyes, my husband was on his knees praying to God to NOT take me from him.[1]

Marcy and her husband overcame their marriage struggles and became parents as God had told her they would.

The compassion and comfort God gives to his children are incomparable to any other, and he wants you to feel his presence during the hardship and pain you experience in life. As believers, we have been given God's Spirit to live in us, pour his love into our hearts, and help us endure by giving us truth on which to stand (John 14:16–17).

When you are in seasons of suffering, draw near to Jesus, and he will give you a renewed perspective to hold on to during the struggle. Jesus identifies with your suffering, and he wants to comfort you with empathy and compassion. He cares about your every concern, no matter how big or small. Today, allow yourself to be comforted by the One who knows and loves you most.

Prayer: *Dear Father, thank you for the comfort and compassion you give me through Jesus. Help me draw near to you in all my suffering and trials.*

18

I will sing of the LORD's great love forever; with my mouth
I will make your faithfulness known through all generations.

Psalm 89:1

MUSIC IS LIKE WATER TO THE SOUL. There's something
mysterious about the way it moves us, and we seem to
need it. And have you ever thought about how many
love songs have been written? Maybe this constant expression of
love put to music is just a shadow of the eternal songs of Heaven.

The music of Heaven is one of the most noted features of NDEs.
Even though some songs are recognized, as Don Piper explained,
they are experienced in a new dimension.

> The music was my most vivid memory. Imagine hearing every dif-
> ferent genre, from Bach to Queen, all at the same time. There
> were so many thousands of songs at the same time without any
> sense of chaos. They were all glorifying God, of course, but there
> was no chaos amongst the songs, even though they were all being
> offered at the same time. You could hear each one of the songs
> with your ears, heavenly ears. That music kind of penetrated me,
> it kind of invaded me to the point that I came back with it and I
> can still hear it today.[1]

Betty Malz describes joining in the chorus:

> We walked along in silence save for the whisper of a gentle breeze
> ruffling the white, sheer garments of the angel. We came upon
> a magnificent, silver structure. It was like a palace except there
> were no towers. As we walked toward it, I heard voices. They were
> melodious, harmonious, blending in chorus and I heard the word,
> "Jesus." There were more than four parts to their harmony. I not
> only heard the singing and felt the singing but I joined the singing.

I have always had a girl's body, but a low boy's voice. Suddenly I realized I was singing the way I had always wanted to . . . in high, clear, and sweet tones. After a while the music softened, then the unseen voices picked up a new chorus.[2]

Dale felt overwhelmed with love when he heard Heaven's harmonies:

Perhaps this is what love sounds like when put to music. It felt so. And every part of me felt it. I was in complete harmony with it, and it accompanied me, beguiling me onward throughout my journey. I thought I would burst with exuberance as I found myself included in such sacred and joyous melodies.[3]

Throughout generations and in every musical genre, love songs have permeated cultures across the globe. Perhaps it is because people long for loving relationships, and these love songs reflect an ultimate longing for the love song of Heaven. But unlike the songs popular on earth, God's love songs offer no heartbreaks, betrayals, or tears. Only unconditional love, acceptance, and joy are found in his presence!

Imagine the day when all music will reflect your heart's experience of Heaven's unconditional love, and nothing will be bittersweet or heartbreaking as you listen and sing along. Instead, the songs you hear will simply delight your heart and forever satisfy your soul's deepest longings.

As you hear your favorite songs today, let them connect your soul to their real source—your Heavenly Father's perfect love. Let every love song be an opportunity to sing of the Lord's great love for you and your love for him.

> **Prayer:** *Dear Father in Heaven, thank you for the music that brings joy to my heart. As I hear love songs today, help me connect them to you, the ultimate Source of all love.*

19

God is light; in him there is no darkness at all.

1 John 1:5

JAYA'S GRANDFATHER was the Hindu guru for his village. At the age of twelve, Jaya wanted to know if the gods were real, so he broke into his grandfather's locked chest containing the ancient Vedic scriptures written on palm leaves. In the Rigveda (the oldest of the Hindu scriptures), he read about the god of light, the creator of all, who came as the Purush Prajapati, "the Lord of all creation who became Man," and sacrificed himself to pay so that we could be freed from the effects of karma (payback for good and bad deeds).[1] Something inside made Jaya determined to find out about this god of light.

The Hindu priest told young Jaya that if he wanted to see the god of light, he must immerse himself in the Krishna River every night for one hundred nights and chant a special mantra one hundred thousand times. If he did this perfectly, the god of light would appear.

Undaunted, Jaya spent the next three months chest-deep in the filth and human sewage floating down the river. One hundred thousand mantras later, Jaya crawled out onto the bank of the river, waiting for the god of light to appear. No light appeared except the distant light of the rising moon. Jaya was extremely discouraged, and he gave up the search for two years.

At age sixteen, Jaya asked a holy man about the god of light. This guru told Jaya he would take him to a Hindu high priest who lived eight hundred miles away, who knew the god of light. Jaya decided to secretly run away with this holy man to see the high priest, willing to face the consequences when he returned.

Halfway through the weeklong train ride, Jaya discovered the holy man and his assistant had disappeared, and with them all

Jaya's possessions and money. Jaya got kicked off the train for having no ticket. Too ashamed to return home, too dismayed to hope, despair set in as he decided to end his life.

Jaya laid his body across the train tracks. In one last prayer of desperation he cried, "God of light, if you are real, reveal yourself to me now, for I am about to take my life." Suddenly a light appeared—Jaya thought at first it was the light of an oncoming train, but it was brighter than any light he'd ever seen. A voice from the light said, "Jaya, I am the God you are seeking. I am the God of light. My name is Jesus."

Jaya came to faith in Jesus, the God of light, before he ever met a Christian or saw a Bible. For the last twenty-five years, he and his wife have served among the poorest in India, starting an orphanage, providing job skills for women at risk, founding a hospital, and planting churches to help others in his country know the God of light.[2]

Jesus is the God of light, love, and forgiveness. He wants all people from all nations to turn to him, and he responds when we seek him with all our hearts. He has put eternity in every human heart, and he will always be found by those who truly seek him in whatever way they know how.

As believers, we are the light of the world. And we can shine brightly and boldly for Christ, loving people and serving them as he did on earth. As we radiate his love, his light will dispel the darkness and will illuminate the ways God wants to shine his blessing on the world. He will do that through you as you are willing!

Let his light shine through your words of encouragement and acts of kindness today, and you will feel the joy and blessing it brings. What an honor to be able to proactively take part in what God is doing in the world to bring all nations into his Heavenly kingdom!

> **Prayer:** *God of light, thank you for seeking and saving the lost, including me. Help me to shine your light to the world and bring more people into your kingdom.*

20

And now . . . we want you to know what will happen to the believers who have died so you will not grieve like people who have no hope.

1 Thessalonians 4:13 NLT

Four-year-old Colton Burpo had a brush with death and claimed to visit Heaven. Several months later, he and his dad, Todd, were driving across the Nebraska cornfields. Colton asked Todd if he had a grandpa named Pop. Todd said he did and told Colton that Pop had passed away when Todd was about Colton's age.

Colton replied, "He's really nice."

Todd almost drove off the road. He later relates, "It's a crazy moment when your son uses the present tense to refer to someone who died a quarter century before he was even born." As Todd and Colton continued to talk, Colton explained that he not only met Pop in Heaven, but he got to stay with him.[1]

Not long after they got back from their road trip, Todd pulled out the last picture of Pop he had. Pop was sixty-two, with white hair and glasses. Todd asked if Colton recognized him. Colton squinched up his face, shook his head, and said, "Dad, nobody's old in heaven . . . and nobody wears glasses." It bothered Todd that Colton didn't recognize Pop, so he had his mom send a younger picture of Pop when he was twenty-nine, standing with his wife and two other people. He showed it to Colton, who said, "Hey! How did you get a picture of Pop?"[2]

Colton's great-grandmother, whom Colton had recently seen, was also pictured next to Pop. Colton didn't recognize his great-grandmother in her twenties, yet he recognized his twenty-nine-year-old great-grandfather he'd never met!

Later that October, Colton gave his family another surprise. "Mommy, I have two sisters," Colton said. His mom, Sonja, corrected him, reminding him he only had one sister. Colton repeated himself, insisting that he had two sisters. Sonja replied that Cassie is his only sister, and then asked if he meant his cousin, Traci.

"No!" Colton insisted adamantly. "I have two sisters. You had a baby die in your tummy, didn't you?" Shocked, Sonja asked her son who it was that told him that.

"She did, Mommy," Colton explained. "She said she died in your tummy." Sonja was overcome with emotion. They had never told Colton about the miscarriage. "It's okay, Mommy," Colton said. "God adopted her." Sonja asked him what her name was. "She doesn't have a name. You guys didn't name her." "You're right, Colton," Sonja said, dumbfounded. "We didn't even know she was a she." Colton said, "Yeah, she said she just can't wait for you and Daddy to get to heaven."[3]

Imagine all the family losses finally redeemed by the love of God. Imagine all the little babies finally reunited with their families, all the brothers and sisters, moms and dads, grandparents, and even distant relatives joined together as a family inside God's great Family.

If you are missing a loved one, hold on to the hope that you will be reunited again, and let that anticipation bring you joy in the waiting. There will be a glorious reunion one day that will be celebrated for all eternity! Death will be no more, never again separating us from those we love.

Today, think of how exhilarating it will be when you see your loved ones again in the life to come! Knowing the joy that is coming when you will be with them again can bring comfort and peace to your heart now, even as you miss their physical presence in this life.

Prayer: *Dear Heavenly Father, thank you that earthly death is not the end of life. Help me hold on to the joy I will experience forever in heaven with loved ones I miss here on earth.*

There before me was a great multitude that no one could count, from every nation, tribe, people and language, standing before the throne and before the Lamb [Jesus]. They were wearing white robes and were holding palm branches in their hands.

Revelation 7:9

Bank president Marv Besteman saw the diversity of people that made up Heaven's community:

The smiling people who stood in that line were from all over the world and wore all kinds of different clothing. I saw many different nationalities represented, including Scandinavian, Asian, African, and Middle Eastern . . . [as well as] primitive African tribes; they were wearing loose, flowing tribal gowns and toga-like garb with sandals on their feet. . . .

Standing in a short line of people, I observed the other thirty-five or so heavenly travelers, people of all nationalities. Some were dressed in what I thought were probably the native costumes of their lands. One man carried a baby in his arms. . . .

I saw huge white pillars surrounding the throne, and an enormous crowd of people, men and women, boys and girls, dancing and singing along in a mass choir of praise.[1]

Betty Malz recalls hearing beautiful harmonies sung in many diverse languages:

The voices not only burst forth in more than four parts, but they were in different languages. I was awed by the richness and perfect blending of the words—and I could understand them! I do not know why this was possible except that I was part of a universal experience. . . . We all seemed to be on some universal wave length.

I thought at the time, *I will never forget the melody and these words*. But later I could only recall two: "Jesus" and "redeemed."[2]

Mary Neal had an interesting observation when she saw Jesus:

I would say that just like the colors of the pathway, it was as though his hair, his eyes, his skin, were all the colors simultaneously. . . . And that made sense to me at the time, because if you look around any room—let alone any part of the world—there are so many hair colors, eye colors, skin shades. We are all created beings, and why wouldn't we all be reflected in him?[3]

Every human is created in the image of God, and he loves us all the same. It is fascinating to look around at all the nationalities, races, cultures, and personalities of men and women across the globe, knowing that God's image is more fully represented by our diversities than any one type alone. Heaven will be a beautiful mosaic of people making up its community!

So often, even unintentionally, we limit our perception of God to the preferences of our own ethnicity, gender, language, or culture. This restricts our understanding of the great richness of God's image. All humanity—every tribe, tongue, and nation, both male and female—reflects him, and all people are important in radiating and displaying the fullness of the image of God.

As you see the nations represented in your neighborhood, church, school, and workplace, take time to appreciate these people as reflections of God's image. Today, think about opportunities you can create to develop friendships and community with people of other backgrounds, races, and cultures. This delights the heart of God.

Prayer: *Dear Father, help me to view all people as a reflection of your true image. Show me how I can demonstrate interest and value to someone different from me today, learning more about you as a result.*

22

You keep track of all my sorrows. You have collected all my tears in your bottle. You have recorded each one in your book.

Psalm 56:8 NLT

BEFORE HER NDE, the concept of God as a loving Father made no sense to Crystal. Why didn't he protect her when the sexual abuse began? Why would he allow all the pain caused by her father's leaving, all the suffering from an abusive stepfather, and all the chaos of a partying mother who left her with questionable company?

Later, Crystal went to the hospital for pancreatitis. Due to complications, she died for nine minutes and found herself in Heaven.

> I was instantly aware of two beings in front of me and to my left, and I knew right away who they were—they were angels. But they weren't just any angels—they were my angels. I recognized them immediately . . . as if they had been by my side for every tear I ever cried, every decision I had ever made, every day I ever felt lonely . . . [I] felt an immediate connection, a sense of deep communication with them, and a complete lack of shame, secrets, misunderstanding, or negativity. Instead, there was only a deep, beautiful, sustaining sense of knowing.

As she stood in front of them, an immense love for these beings swept through her. The angels felt like the closest friends she could ever have. Crystal also sensed another profusion of brightness coming from a Being on her right, whom she knew without a doubt was God. She was immediately overcome with a profound desire to worship him. Although she had always referred to God as a him, she understood that God was neither a him nor a her, but simply God, and that God, Jesus, and the Holy Spirit "were all One—the One before me now."

Crystal had put her faith in Christ as a child, but all the evil she endured had caused her to doubt.

> I'd spent my life doubting His existence and disbelieving His love for me, but in that instant I knew God had always, always been there—right there with me. . . . And you know, back on Earth, I had so many questions for God. "If I ever meet Him," I'd say, "I'm going to ask Him how He could let someone molest me when I was a child. How could He abide brutality against children or the suffering of starving people or cruelty toward the weak?" . . . In His presence I absolutely understood that in every way God's plan is perfect. Sheer, utter perfection.
>
> Does that mean I can now explain how [it all] fits into God's plan? No. I understood it in heaven, but we aren't meant to have that kind of understanding here on Earth. All I can tell you is that I know God's plan is perfect. In His radiance, it all makes perfect, perfect sense. In this way all the questions I had for God were answered without me even having to ask them.[1]

God is a compassionate, merciful God. He abhors the evil in the world and cannot cause it, although he allows people to make choices against his will in their own free will.

God is our Heavenly Father, and he identifies with the sufferings of his children. He collects every tear that falls down your cheeks, and cares deeply about your emotional pain. You are of immeasurable value to him, and he wants to walk with you through your struggles with unwavering, unfailing love.

Even though it is difficult on this side of Heaven to make sense of suffering, in his sovereignty God will take what Satan meant for evil and redeem it for good. One day you will understand how. Lean on him today, cry on his shoulder, for God is here to comfort you whenever you call.

> **Prayer:** *Heavenly Father, it's hard to understand why bad things happen to so many people—including me. But I do know that you love me and will walk with me through the trials to make something good of them as I trust in you.*

23

If you hold to my teaching, you are really my disciples. Then
you will know the truth, and the truth will set you free.

John 8:31–32

GROWING UP, Crystal had suffered abuse at the hands of
evil men. As a result, evil successfully planted lies in her
psyche about her worth and value. In Heaven, God helped
Crystal replace the lies and wounds inflicted by evil with his truth.
He showed her a beautiful three-year-old girl playing with an Easter basket.

> She wore a bonnet on her head and she had a little white basket in
> her hand. I watched her pick her basket up and dip it in the light.
> She would scoop it and then she would dump the light out as if it
> was water. And the light would cascade out of her basket and she
> would throw her head back. And she would laugh. And every time
> she laughed, every time she moved, my spirit began to swell, as if
> it was a balloon with love.

Watching the little girl play with the Easter basket prompted
an immense feeling of love and pride in Crystal's spirit. The feeling grew and intensified, "radiating waves of love" that were so
deep, intense, and endless, she felt her soul would burst. Crystal
remembers wanting nothing more than to run toward the little
girl, embrace her, and tell her how much she loved her.

Suddenly, God revealed to Crystal that *she* was the little girl
with the golden Easter basket. Because she had been three years
old when her abuse began, God took Crystal back to that very age.

> [The little girl] was me at the moment the enemy stepped into my
> life and whispered that I was worthless, that I was broken, that I
> was disgusting, and that I got everything I deserved. She was the

3-year-old that heard that God didn't love her, that He had abandoned her, that He had forsaken her, and that God didn't exist. And, He had allowed me to look through His eyes and to see the truth. And the truth set me free.[1]

In God's eyes, Crystal was perfect, washed clean by Jesus's sacrifice on the cross. That would never change, no matter what happened to her on earth, and no matter what bad decisions had been made that had filled her with a sense of worthlessness. Before this happened, Crystal believed God couldn't possibly love her, but now she knew she had based her beliefs on a lie—a lie God obliterated with his love.[2]

You don't have to wait for Heaven to be set free. Standing on the promises of God can set you free right now! The way you fight evil is with God's truth—taking thoughts captive, resisting the lies you hear in your mind, and standing firm, trusting God's truth alone.

You are God's masterpiece, his wonderful creation, his precious child. He loves you more than you can imagine, and that love has no conditions or bounds attached. Believing anything less can imprison you and keep you from living the life he desires for you.

You can live free as you trust in the promises of God's steadfast love for you. He wants you to experience his peace and presence every moment. No matter how distant from God you have felt in the past, let today be the start of letting God's truth set you free to know and feel how loved you really are!

> **Prayer:** *Jesus, I want to stand firm in your truth and resist any lies from the evil one that keep me from experiencing your unconditional love. I am your child, and you love me more than I can imagine. Help me to live in light of that truth and be set free.*

24

So now there is no condemnation for those who belong to Christ Jesus.

Romans 8:1 NLT

PROFESSOR HOWARD STORM was an atheist most of his adult life, and during his NDE found himself in a brutally abusive hellish experience. He described what happened next:

And as I'm thinking . . . "There's no hope. There's no way out," I am in the bottom of the pit of hopelessness and despair and self-pity . . . this memory comes of myself as a little boy, sitting in a Sunday school classroom singing "Jesus Loves Me." And I could see myself vividly: so innocent, so sweet, so naive, simple. And feeling what I felt when I was like a little boy, maybe eight or nine years old. "Jesus loves me, this I know." That's what I kept hearing over and over again. . . .

But more important than the words was what I felt as a little boy. This simple, this beautiful Superman figure—better than Superman—loved me, cared about me. And when I prayed to him, he took care of me. And you know, the alligators under the bed and the bears in the closet and the witches in the halls and all those things that you're afraid of when you're a little boy, I had prayed to Jesus and they would go away, they'd stop. . . .

But I had put all that away behind me . . . and denied it all and mocked it all. And now, all of a sudden it was all I had. I had nothing else. I'm scraping the bottom of the barrel of what might be possible, so I thought . . . "Enough of this! I'm done! I don't have anything else. Jesus, please save me!"

And when I said that, I saw a light. A tiny, little speck of light, and it rapidly got very bright and came over me. And I saw hands and arms emerge out of this impossibly beautiful light . . . and they reached and they touched me. And in that light . . . all the gore began to just dissolve, and I became whole. And much more significant to me than the physical healing was that I was experiencing a love that is . . . far beyond words. I have never been able to articulate it, but I can say that if I took all my experience of love in my entire life and could condense it into a moment, it still wouldn't begin to measure up to the intensity of this love that I was feeling.

And when those arms went on me and healed me, they went behind my back and he picked me up as if it was no effort on his part. He just gently picked me up and held me up against him real tight, up against his chest. So there I am, with my arms around him, his arms around me. And I am [sobbing] with my head buried in his chest . . . like a mom or dad with a child.[1]

Howard remembers they rose up through space toward a large illuminated area in the distance. Howard found himself thinking:

I am a terrible piece of garbage. They should put me back where I belong, back in that hole of darkness and terror. They made a terrible mistake. I belong back there. "We don't make mistakes," he [Jesus] said. "You belong here." . . . I knew. I knew that he loved me very much, just the way I was.[2]

Because Howard hadn't fully crossed over the boundary from life to death, he was still able to call out to Jesus. "Everyone who calls on the name of the Lord will be saved" (Rom. 10:13).

God doesn't make mistakes. He loves every person he ever created—even when they reject him—and he longs for all of his children to be with him for eternity. You could never drift too far out of God's loving reach. No matter what you have done, Jesus will rescue you when you call out his name. You will not be condemned, but you will be forgiven through the blood of Jesus shed for you. If you haven't yet, open up your heart to Jesus today.

Prayer: *Lord Jesus, thank you that I do not stand condemned but am forgiven through your blood shed for me.*

25

We must all appear before the judgment seat of Christ, so that each of us may receive what is due us for the things done while in the body, whether good or bad.

2 Corinthians 5:10

AFTER HOWARD CRIED TO JESUS from the outskirts of hell and was rescued, Jesus asked him if he wished to view his life. Unsure of what to expect, Howard agreed. Here's how he described the life review:[1]

There are these angels in a semicircle around us. . . . Jesus wanted them to play out, in chronological order, the scenes of my life. Mine was not as some people describe: panoramic, instantaneous. Mine was chronological from when I was born up to the present, moment by moment, life by life . . . in detail, including knowing, experiencing the feelings of the people that I was interacting with. . . . The entire emphasis was on my interaction with other people—of course, initially starting out with my mother and father, my sisters . . . school and friends.

The whole emphasis was on people and not on things. . . . As my life progressed, my adolescence into adulthood, I saw myself turning completely away from God, church, all that, and becoming a person who decided that life was all about [being] the biggest, baddest bear in the woods. . . .

As a matter of fact, there were some instances where I had won promotions, honors, awards [as a college professor], and they skipped them. And I said to Jesus, "You're skipping the most important thing in my life! This is what I lived for, to get this award! Kentucky Artist of the Year: big banquet in my honor and a big cash prize and everything." And he said, "That's not what we're here for you to see. That's not important. What I want you to see is how you treated the students."

Howard could barely watch some of the scenes from his life as they were replayed by the angels, even though Jesus and the angels were not condemning but comforting him.

> And now I began to experience Jesus's and the angels' literal pain, emotional pain with watching the sins in my life. . . . I had not been the father to my kids that I should have been, and I knew I hadn't—because I was busy. I was trying to be somebody. . . .
>
> [Their] football games and the band concerts and the choral concerts and the theater performances; they could all wait, because I was busy being important. I was doing stuff making myself into somebody. The emotional abandonment of my children was devastating to review.[2]
>
> Here's the nicest, kindest, most loving being I've ever met who, I realized, is my Lord, my Savior, even my Creator; holding me and supporting me, trying to give me more understanding of my life. And the last thing I want to do is to hurt him, and I don't want to hurt him to this day. Jesus is a very feeling man. God is a very feeling Creator.

The life review clarifies what really matters to God, as he shows people that every little action has relational reverberation, person to person, for good or for bad. How we choose to treat other people is close to God's heart, and the effects of our kindnesses upon others can have lasting impact.

The love and acceptance Jesus bestows upon us is not conditional nor will it ever change. As Ephesians 2:8–9 says, salvation is a gift! But this does not negate the reality that our choices on earth do matter, and we will be rewarded for every noble and loving act of kindness. Love and kindness reflect the heart of God. Today, bring joy and delight to God's heart by the actions you show toward the people he has put in your life.

> **Prayer:** *Lord, help me to live my life each day in light of my future life review. Not out of fear of punishment, but out of desire to delight you and participate in what brings you joy.*

26

I have loved you even as the Father has loved me. Remain in my love. . . . This is my commandment: Love each other in the same way I have loved you.

John 15:9, 12 NLT

IT WAS 1943 IN CAMP BARKLEY, Texas, and George Ritchie had enlisted to fight the Nazis. In the middle of boot camp, he woke up at midnight, heart pounding, with a 106-degree fever. During X-rays, he passed out. The attending doctor declared him dead. Years later as a medical doctor, George would display his death certificate whenever he spoke about his life-changing encounter.

"Where was I?" George pondered.

I stared in astonishment as the brightness increased, coming from nowhere, seeming to shine everywhere at once. . . . It was impossibly bright: it was like a million welders' lamps all blazing at once. And right in the middle of my amazement came a prosaic thought, probably born of some biology lecture back at the university: "I'm glad I don't have physical eyes at this moment," I thought. "This light would destroy the retina in a tenth of a second."

No, I corrected myself, not the light.

He.

He would be too bright to look at. For now I saw that it was not light but a Man who had entered the room, or rather, a Man made out of light. . . .

The instant I perceived Him, a command formed itself in my mind. "Stand up!" . . . I got to my feet, and as I did came the stupendous certainty: You are in the presence of the Son of God. . . . [From His presence came] a love beyond my wildest imagining. This love knew every unlovable thing about me—every mean, selfish thought and action since the day I was born—and accepted and loved me just the same. . . .

He was not blaming or reproaching. He was simply loving me. Filling the world with Himself and yet somehow attending to me personally. Waiting for my answer to the question that still hung in the dazzling air. *What have you done with your life to show Me?*. . . The question, like everything else proceeding from Him, had to do with love. How much have you loved with your life?[1]

Whatever I saw was only—from the doorway, so to speak. But it was enough to convince me totally . . . that how we spend our time on earth, the kind of relationships we build, is vastly, infinitely more important than we can know.[2]

You are lavishly and unconditionally loved by Jesus! Despite all you have done, failed to do, or are struggling with now, you are fully and completely loved. There is nothing you could ever do to change the immense love God feels for you, just as you are. This is the truth about you, and the way God wired you to live. "Like an eagle is made to soar the heights, we were made for God's love. Love is our native atmosphere."[3]

Sometimes you may hear thoughts in your head telling you that you are not worthy. Reject them—they are lies! Instead, focus on staying connected to God's love every moment of every day, as Jesus encourages in the words of John 15:9 above. As you do this, he will infuse his love into your heart and mind and then into your relationships, helping you extend this same merciful love toward the people he puts in your path.

Today, as God fills you up with his love, find creative ways to share his love with others in your life. Watch how this will not only transform you but also be a life-giving force to others through you.

Prayer: *Heavenly Father, thank you for the amazing, unconditional, incomparable love of Jesus. Help me to receive it and remain in it today, empowering me to love others the same way that you love me.*

27

Holy, holy, holy is the LORD Almighty; the whole earth is full of his glory.

Isaiah 6:3

D<small>R. RICHARD EBY</small> considered himself an amateur botanist, but he couldn't even name all the varieties of trees and flowers he saw during his NDE. He also noticed a new type of life in the flora:

> My gaze riveted on the exquisite valley in which I found myself. Forests of symmetrical trees unlike anything on earth covered the foothills on each side. I could see each branch and "leaf"—not a brown spot or dead leaf in the forest. ("No death there" includes the vegetation!) Each tree, tall and graceful, was a duplicate of the others; perfect, unblemished. They resembled somewhat the tall arbor vitae cedars of North America, but I could not identify them.
>
> The valley floor was gorgeous. Stately grasses, each blade perfect and erect, were interspersed with ultra-white, four-petalled flowers on stems two feet tall, with a touch of gold at the centers. Each was totally alike. . . .
>
> Having been an amateur botanist as a schoolboy, I immediately decided to pick a bouquet. To my amazement the unexpected happened. My thought (to stoop and pick flowers) became the act! Here in Paradise, I discovered that there is no time lag between thought and act. A word, spoken or thought, became fact! (I instantly realized how the heavens and earth were so quickly made from nothing that appeared: God had simply thought what He wanted, and there it was. No sluggish man-invented committees were involved.)
>
> I found my hand containing a bouquet of identical blossoms. Their whiteness was exciting. I almost had time to ask myself "why so white" when the answer was already given! "On earth you saw only white light which combined the color spectrum of the sun.

Here we have the light of the SON!" My excitement was too great to describe in words: of course, I thought He is the light of the world. . . . In the new Heavens no sun or moon will be needed! Then I sensed a strange new feel to the stems—no moisture! I felt them carefully. Delicately smooth, yet nothing like earthly stems with their cellular watery content. Before I could ask, again I had the answer: earthly water is hydrogen and oxygen for temporary life support; here Jesus is the Living Water. . . .

The illumination fascinated me—not a shadow anywhere. There was no single light source as on earth. I realized that everything seemed to produce its own light. Again the answer coincided with my query: the Heavens declare the glory of God . . . He is the Light of the world![1]

The language of Scripture and the words NDErs use over and over again emphasize that our temporal, earthly life is the fuzzy, less-than-real shadow of the brilliant, beautiful, beyond-your-wildest-dreams, real life to come. As Isaiah 6:3 says, the earth is displaying God's glory even now. Our sun is simply a reminder of the radiance of God, who is the Light of life, and our water is a reminder of the living water of God's Holy Spirit.

One day you will experience living water flowing through all of Heaven's beauty. And right now, Jesus promises that when you thirst for him, you can drink in his living water, the joy of his Spirit. And his shining light will lead and guide you on your journey as you follow him.

As you go about your day today, be mindful of God's glory reflected in all of earth's beauty, and praise him for these gifts he's given you to enjoy. You can experience his brilliant glory now, as you worship him.

Prayer: *Dear God, I am in awe of you! Help me worship you today as I encounter your glory all around me.*

28

The LORD doesn't see things the way you see them. People judge by outward appearance, but the LORD looks at the heart.

1 Samuel 16:7 NLT

JEFF HAD A BRUSH WITH DEATH when his car rolled seven times. Just before he returned to his body from his NDE, the oneness he experienced in Heaven gave him insight into the people walking past in the hospital. Though they could not see him, he saw into them in a surprisingly new way:

I knew each person I saw perfectly. I knew their joys and their sorrows. I knew their love, their hate, their pain, and their secrets. I knew everything about them, every detail, every motivation, and every outcome. I knew every emotion they were feeling, and I knew intuitively why they were feeling it. In an instant, with no contemplation, I knew them as well as I knew myself. I knew their hearts.

I looked into the face of a woman in her early thirties and felt her elation at the anticipated marriage proposal from her boyfriend. I instantly knew that this was the second time around for her, but also that this was Mr. Right. I watched as a man in his late forties approached me. I felt his guilt over words he'd had with his brother. I saw how his pride would never allow him to take it back or apologize, and how that disjointed him spiritually. He was literally splitting in two between remorse and arrogance.

Another woman walked toward me from the opposite direction. She quickly looked down as she passed. It was almost as if she saw me. I experienced her pain from the abuse she had received as a child. I saw how broken it made her feel. I felt how damaged and unworthy she had viewed herself for years and how she still felt that way. At the same time, I also felt her capacity to love and her strength because of what she had been through. I saw how her compassion was being drowned out by her shame. . . .

What if I could feel every person's hurt and joy and know every motivation and reason for his or her every action or thought? What if I could feel the unconditional love I was now experiencing for every soul? I marveled at my perceptions. Most of my life I had actually avoided people. . . .

Words Jesus had said rushed to my recollection: "Inasmuch as ye have done it unto the least of these my brethren ye have done it unto me." Was he talking about the awareness I was experiencing? Did he feel the same thing I was feeling? Was this how he walked the earth, in the consciousness of knowing each individual soul at this deep level of love? . . . We are all linked and equal in God's eyes. I was seeing it, feeling it, and experiencing it.[1]

When we truly look at people through Jesus's eyes, we see past the exterior that often distracts or even triggers us, and into their hearts, where their spiritual needs and insecurities reside. The love and empathy that Jesus has for each of us, and the mercy and compassion he gives to all of his children, are what we desperately need more of in the world.

At times it may be hard to care for others when we feel wounded too, and some of us may have many hurts and scars. However, as Philo of Alexandria said over two thousand years ago, "Be kind, for everyone you meet is fighting a great battle." No one is immune to the struggles that life brings, and everyone faces challenges that others know nothing about. Let this motivate us to reach out and extend the same kindness and grace to others we long to receive.

As you think of the people God has put into your life, ask him to show you new ways to encourage and minister to them. Today, focus on seeing people through Jesus's eyes, past the exterior and into their hearts, and feel God's love grow in yours.

> **Prayer:** *Dear God, help me see others the way you see them. Fill me with your lovingkindness and compassion toward their pain.*

29

With the Lord a day is like a thousand years, and a thousand years are like a day.

2 Peter 3:8

O N November 10, 2008, Harvard neurosurgeon Eben Alexander was struck by a rare illness, causing his entire neocortex—the part of the brain that makes us human—to shut down. What he experienced reversed the conclusions he'd formed through medical school. He felt alive like never before, and experienced a world far more expansive in time and space than we could ever conceive.

He found himself flying over a green, idyllic landscape that seemed very much like earth, yet different at the same time. He talks candidly about his NDE in a live interview:

> I remember ascending up into this brilliant, ultra-real valley . . . this brilliant greenery lush with life. . . . I remember how we would dip down and go through that lush greenery, and there would be flowers and blossoms and buds on trees that would open up even as we flew by. I remember the rich textures and colors beyond the rainbow.
>
> In that beautiful valley, as we would come up and ascend above all that greenery, I could see . . . hundreds of souls dancing. I describe them as being dressed in peasant garb—very simple clothing, yet beautiful colors, and tremendous joy and merriment, and there were lots of children playing . . . It was just a wonderful festival!
>
> And it was all being fueled because up above—in the velvety skies above—were pure spiritual beings [angels, he later thought], orbs of golden light, swooping and swirling in formation leaving sparkling golden trails, emanating these hymns, chants, anthems—powerful like a tsunami wave, crescendo after crescendo of the most beautiful music. Waves washing through me—and that's what was fueling this incredible joy and mirth going on in this gateway valley. . . .

The important thing to understand is this gateway valley was much more real than this world—far sharper, crisper, more real than this—this [world] is very dream-like by comparison. That was a deep, deep mystery to me for a long time, trying to understand that ultra-reality.[1]

When you go to a place where there's no sense of time as we experience it in the ordinary world, accurately describing the way it feels is next to impossible. . . . I saw that there are countless higher dimensions, but that the only way to know these dimensions is to enter and experience them directly. . . . Cause and effect exist in these higher realms, but outside of our earthly conception of them. The world of time and space in which we move in this [earthly] terrestrial realm is tightly and intricately meshed within these higher worlds. . . . From those higher worlds one could access any time or place in our world.[2]

How comforting to know that God is not bound by reality as we experience it on earth! And our true reality is the one where God resides. There are no limits to all he can accomplish in us and through us in his heavenly time frame, for it has no earthly bounds.

You can trust him in your day by day, moment by moment experiences, as he sees all possibilities ahead for you and will carry out his plan for you as you seek him every moment. God's capacities are limitless, and he wants to help carry your burdens and accomplish the tasks before you. "Give all your worries and cares to God, for he cares about you" (1 Peter 5:7 NLT).

Jesus wants to give you joy and beauty in your experience of life with him. And remember, you have enough time to do what he created you to do. Lean on him today, seeking his will and timing for what is best. He is in control, and time is in his hands.

Prayer: *Dear God, it gives me peace to know that you are not bound by earthly limitations or time like I am. Help me commit my days to you, for I know I have enough time to accomplish your will for my life.*

30

Enter his gates with thanksgiving and his courts with praise;
give thanks to him and praise his name.

Psalm 100:4

DON PIPER was about to enter the city gate in Heaven.
Imagine if you were experiencing this rapturous crescendo
of musical joy:

> Everything I saw was bright—the brightest colors my eyes had ever
> beheld—so powerful that no earthly human could take in this bril-
> liance. . . . As we came closer to the gate, the music increased and
> became even more vivid. It would be like walking up to a glorious
> event after hearing the faint sounds and seeing everything from
> a distance. The closer we got, the more intense, alive, and vivid
> everything became. . . . Instead of just hearing the music and the
> thousands of voices praising God, I had become part of the choir.
> I was one with them, and they had absorbed me into their midst.
> I had arrived at a place I had wanted to visit for a long time; I
> lingered to gaze before I continued forward.[1]

Dr. Eben Alexander recalls the angels praising God:

> A sound, huge and booming like a glorious chant, came down
> from above, and I wondered if the winged beings were producing
> it. Again thinking about it later, it occurred to me that the joy of
> these creatures, as they soared along, was such that they had to
> make this noise—that if the joy didn't come out of them this way
> then they would simply not otherwise be able to contain it.[2]

Gary was also caught up in the rapture of this angelic choir:

> You've never heard singing until you hear trillions of angels singing
> to the Lord. This singing meant a lot to me especially because I had

earned a music degree on earth. Being in surround sound with the songs of angels was overwhelming, beyond what I can capture in mortal words to tell you.[3]

Captain Dale Black felt the music of heaven unifying people as if his very being was tuned to the music:

> Somehow the music in heaven calibrated everything. . . . Music was everywhere. The worship of God was the heart and focus of the music, and everywhere the joy of the music could be felt. The deepest part of my heart resonated with it, made me want to be a part of it forever. I never wanted it to stop. . . . I had the feeling— and it was the most satisfying of feelings—that I was made for the music, as if each muscle in my body were a taut string of some finely tuned instrument, created to play the most beautiful music ever composed. I felt part of the music. One with it. Full of joy and wonder and worship. . . . The music of praise seemed to be alive and it passed through me, permeating every cell. My being seemed to vibrate like a divine tuning fork. I felt all this, every ecstatic moment of it. And I never wanted it to end.[4]

The music of Heaven must be spectacular! How awesome it will be to worship and praise God with the angels. Music is a gift from God; it can lift you up and bring peace to your soul. A song can minister to your grieving heart and calm your mind and it can bring joy and happiness to your celebrations and exciting times.

Praise and worship music unites, comforts, reassures, and re-centers believers. It reminds you of God's presence and sovereignty in your life. Today, put a melody in your heart that gives you peace in his presence, and see how it brings joy to your day, "that I might sing praises to you and not be silent. O Lord my God, I will give you thanks forever!" (Ps. 30:12 NLT).

> **Prayer:** *Father, I long to enter your gates with thanksgiving and your courts with praise! Help me to always have a song in my heart of love for you.*

31

"The wolf and the lamb will feed together, and the lion will eat straw like the ox, and dust will be the serpent's food. They will neither harm nor destroy on all my holy mountain," says the LORD.

Isaiah 65:25

IN HEAVEN, it is assuring to know that not only will people we love be there, but our beloved animals and pets will live together in peace and harmony along with us. One near-death experiencer observed:

Flowers grew everywhere, producing a fragrance like sweet-smelling perfume. I marveled at the brilliant colors that the flowers had, each one was different from the other flowers, and no two were alike. . . .

I saw a tiny little girl with long, brown hair that hung in ringlets down her back. She wore a white robe that glistened in the light of our Lord. She had sandals on her small feet. When she saw Jesus, she began to run towards him with her arms stretched out. Jesus stooped down and caught her as she leapt into his arms.

Then from all directions children came running to see Jesus. There were children of every race and color. They all wore robes of white and sandals. . . . While Jesus was ministering to them, all sorts of animals were with the children.

It was an awesome sight to see a magnificent lion frolicking with the children, as if it were a kitten, and seeing birds of elegant beauty sitting on shoulders and tops of heads. I saw teenagers who had left this earth prematurely. They were playing in crystal pools of water, laughing and singing.[1]

Isaiah foresaw God's restoration of all creatures: "The wolf and the lamb will live together. . . . The calf and the yearling will be safe with the lion, and a little child will lead them all" (Isa. 11:6

NLT). Dr. Eben Alexander described seeing children having fun and "dogs jumping."[2]

Researcher Dr. Pim van Lommel discovered that NDE "children do encounter favorite pets that have died more frequently than do adults."[3] A ten-year-old who "died" said, "My pet dog Skippy was there. Skippy had died some years earlier and was the only 'person' that I had any real family connection with that was dead. I was overwhelmed with Joy and Love and embraced my dog."[4]

It is wonderful to imagine that dearly loved pets will be allowed in the Holy City, because all love is of God. God has entrusted to us the stewardship over all his creation, and we are expected to care for all living things on earth as he would.

The way we love and treat our animals counts in God's eyes. This is an act of love for God and should be important to believers. If you have pets, you know how much love they hold in your heart, and your pet loves you back with a loyalty unmatched by most. Our pets are blessings from God. They can teach us about unconditional love and God's desire for our love and loyalty to him.

Today, enjoy your pets as God's gifts to you while on earth. Take delight in knowing that in Heaven, they will share fun and companionship with you along with all of God's creatures.

> **Prayer:** *Father, it's wonderful to imagine my pets and other animals enjoying life forever in harmony with all creatures. Help me love and care for them well here on earth, as they are special gifts from you.*

32

For we are God's masterpiece. He has created us anew in
Christ Jesus, so we can do the good things he planned for
us long ago.

Ephesians 2:10 NLT

So I run with purpose in every step.

1 Corinthians 9:26 NLT

During Gary Wood's NDE, he had a very meaningful
encounter with Jesus, where Jesus talked about purpose
in life.

A radiant, beautiful light came from Him. When He looked at me,
His eyes pierced me, they went all the way through me. Just pure love!
I melted in His presence. [Jesus's] eyes were deep, beautiful pools of
love, and they were blue. I have since learned that Jews from the tribe
of Judah are known to have blue eyes. . . . His words came as the same
sound as the water flowing over Niagara Falls. . . . "Tell people they are
special and unique, each one. God made every one of His children to
have a divine purpose, which only they can accomplish in the earth."[1]

Howard Storm, an atheist professor from Kentucky who cried
out to Jesus during his NDE, shared what he learned in watching
a review of his life with Jesus:

The reason why he didn't love what I did was because it distracted
from who I was meant to be. . . . I was made for one purpose and
one purpose only, and that's what I was missing. . . . I'm not here
to prove anything. I'm simply here to do the very best that I can
with the talents and abilities and gifts that God has given me. . . .
And what I understood was how much he loved me, how much he
cared about me, and how much he liked me just the way I was. One
of the things that people don't understand (that I was given at the

time): he made me. I'm his work, including my mind, including this world. He's the maker, he's the creative activity of God, and he doesn't make junk. He makes good stuff and he cares about what he makes, and he had made me to be a wonderful person. And when I asked him about my flaws or my feelings and my doubts and all this stuff, we talked about all these things. And he finally explained to me that those were to make me, to give me a stronger faith, to give me a stronger relationship with him. And I had used them to drive a huge barrier between him and me.[2]

God has a special and unique plan for each person he has created—including you! You are his unique masterpiece. He wants you to live that way, confident that with him, your life will have meaning and purpose that will be more glorious than anything earth deems important.

Love is central to your purpose, since Love is who God is. You can be confident that as you love God and love people with the gifts God has given you, his purposes will naturally flow from your life.

Don't ever believe the lies that you are not important and that you don't have as much to offer as others. You are of utmost importance to God, and you have something to offer that no one else on the planet can accomplish like you can. In fact, God has already planned good works for you to walk in to make a unique impact on the world (see Eph. 2:10).

Today, focus on how special you are to God. Commit to seeking his will and walking in the works he has planned for you, and see your purpose unfold.

> **Prayer:** *Heavenly Father, it is so wonderful to know that you see me as a masterpiece created by you and unlike any other. Guide me in your ways and in the good works you have already planned for me, so that I fulfill my purpose in this life.*

33

Then they cried to the LORD in their trouble, and he saved them from their distress. He brought them out of darkness, the utter darkness, and broke away their chains. Let them give thanks to the LORD for his unfailing love and his wonderful deeds for mankind.

Psalm 107:13–15

TRACY HAD BEEN THROUGH HELL ON EARTH, and due to choices she'd made to cope, she found herself in bondage:

Prior to my NDE, I was in a terrible situation with a man that was extremely evil. There were days that when he wasn't at the house I would turn on my one Christian CD and get on my knees and cry out to God to help me change and to give me direction. During the five years leading up to my NDE, I was doing things that I felt were killing me on the inside. In fact, I felt dead inside.

I had decided to end that relationship. . . . I admitted myself into [a hospital] for medical help withdrawing from Vicodin. Almost immediately, as the doctor was going to inject some medication to start the withdrawal, I felt a rectangular pain form across my chest. . . . I said aloud, "I can't breathe out." Then, total blackness. I died.

I have no recollection of what occurred in that room when I went unconscious. All of the sudden I was surrounded by pure, bright, brilliant, Heaven white. It was white, but not earthly white. Seriously, there are no words that can explain the beauty of colors in Heaven. . . .

I was in a cell. It was made of brown metal. I had a tan "potato bag" on my body as a form of clothing. I had brown leather bands, "belts" around my neck, waist, wrists and ankles. I believe at first I was somewhat confused. There was love all around me. Much more love than a person can feel here on earth.

One by one, those thick brown bands fell off. The door to the "cell" opened. I walked out and fell to my knees. I couldn't look up. I knew it was Jesus. I was in the presence of the Lord. It was at that time that we were telepathically communicating. I was asking and crying about things that happened to me from the beginning of my life for the most part. (Incest, emotional abuse, physical abuse, mental abuse, running away starting at about twelve years old to get away from all the abuse. Stranger raped at fourteen. Countless things happened to me, but this might give the reader an idea as to where I came from. Frankly, I believe I was living a hell on earth.)

It was amazing and beautiful. My Savior answered, giving me knowledge and peace about every single thing that had happened to me. Everything. However, He didn't allow me to come back with all of that He revealed to me. What He did, is [that He] sent me back with peace in my spirit. Bondages gone. I am a brand new person on the inside. I have been set completely free of my past. I truly believe that He knew I was on a one way ticket to hell, and because of me crying out to Him he answered my prayers!! That is how much He loves me.[1]

Jesus can set us free and cleanse us of all unrighteousness that falls upon us. Our burdens, resentments, addictions, and striving can feel like chains binding us. We may feel like we can never be free of the imprisonment we feel. But through Christ, we can be free! He has set us free through his blood shed on the cross for us. It may take time, but he will do it.

If you feel like you're living in bondage because of wrongs done to you, release any unforgiveness that seeds resentment in your heart. Ask Jesus to replace the hurts with his love and forgiveness, cleansing you. For wrongs you have done, confess your sins to Jesus. Then make right the sins you have committed against others, asking their forgiveness and seeking restoration.

As you seek Jesus with all your heart, fully willing to obey him, he will lead you out of your prison. Today, call out to God—he has the power to break the chains that bind you and set you free!

Prayer: *Dear Jesus, thank you for cleansing me from all unrighteousness and breaking all my chains through the cross. Lead me and I will obediently follow. Heal me and set me free.*

34

Are not all angels ministering spirits sent to serve those who will inherit salvation?

Hebrews 1:14

ELEVEN-YEAR-OLD JENNIFER was in a severe car accident and left her body. She saw her "limp and lifeless body" beside the man driving her. A spiritual being told her, "His nose is cut off his face; you will need to go back and help him; he is bleeding to death." Jennifer said, "No, let somebody else do it. He will be fine without my help. I do not want to go back down there. No!"

The voice said, "I will tell you what to do. You take off his shirt after you pick his nose up off the floorboard of the car. It will be next to your feet and his right foot. Place his nose on his face, pressing down to stop the bleeding. It's just blood, so do not be afraid. . . . So then, Jennifer, you will begin to walk him up the right side of the road, and a car will come. Tell the man to take you to the nearest hospital."

When Jennifer returned to her body, everything happened as she was told. A car stopped and carried them to the hospital. Even in her youth, she was able to calm both the anxious driver and the man who lost his nose. And there was a happy ending: a skin graft was used to reattach the nose with "barely a scratch left to notice." The astonished emergency room doctor said, "I cannot explain what kind of miracle I just witnessed in this emergency room today."[1]

Bank executive Marv Besteman also reported seeing angels:

Everyone has a mental picture of angels, and so did I. When I had thought of angels before I actually met one, I pictured them as younger than the beings I saw . . . And no, actually, neither one of them had wings" [though he later saw winged creatures].[2]

Howard experienced the empathy of the angels:

These beings were far brighter than the most powerful searchlight, yet I could look at them with no sense of discomfort. In fact, their radiance penetrated me . . . and it made me feel wonderful . . . they spoke directly to my mind, not through my ears. And they used normal colloquial English. Everything that I thought, they knew immediately. It was in this way that we conversed. [The angels said,] "You're upset. What can we do to help you?" [I said,] "You've got the wrong person. I don't belong here." [They replied,] "You do belong here. . . . We can appear to you in our human form if you wish or in any form you want, so you will be comfortable with us." . . . [I said,] "No. Please don't change into anything for me. You're more beautiful than anything I've ever seen."[3]

Scripture teaches that angels are spirit creatures who live in God's realm, but they can interact with earth in order to serve and minister to people in the will of God. We are not to pray to them or seek their guidance, but we can take comfort in their ministering presence in our daily lives.

Angels are around you, protecting and helping you in ways you may never fully understand. As Hebrews 13:2 says, "Don't forget to show hospitality to strangers, for some who have done this have entertained angels without realizing it!" (NLT).

It is thrilling to think that the heavenly realm may be even closer to us than we imagine. Today, thank God for the presence of his angels protecting you and your loved ones, and be aware that those strangers you meet on your journey may actually be angels sent from God for a purpose in your life.

> **Prayer:** *Lord, thank you for the ministering presence of your angels and their involvement in my life. Help me to be aware of ways I can show hospitality to others, knowing I may be interacting with angels you bring along my path.*

35

The blind receive sight, the lame walk, those who have leprosy are cleansed, the deaf hear, the dead are raised, and the good news is proclaimed to the poor.

Matthew 11:5

DURING HER NDE, VICKI, who was born blind, noticed that she was fully herself and that she had a distinct form and a nonphysical body she described as "made of light." She had no fear as she found herself moving toward a pinpoint of light getting brighter and brighter.

As she reached where the light was, she heard sublimely beautiful and exquisitely harmonious music that transitioned into songs of praise to God. She was in a place of tremendous light, and the light, Vicki says, "was something you could feel as well as see. . . . Everybody there was made of light. And I was made of light. What the light conveyed was love. There was love everywhere. It was like love came from the grass, love came from the birds, love came from the trees."[1]

Vicki goes on to explain that in Heaven, she was welcomed by some childhood friends who were healthy and whole. Debby and Diane were Vicki's blind schoolmates who had died years before, at ages eleven and six, respectively. In life, they both had severe developmental disabilities, but here they appeared bright and beautiful, healthy and vitally alive. They were no longer children but, as Vicki phrased it, "in their prime."[2]

Brian was born totally deaf, but at age ten he nearly drowned. He recalls the joy of being able to "hear" telepathically in Heaven:

> I approached the boundary. No explanation was necessary for me to understand, at the age of ten, that once I cross[ed] the boundary, I could never come back—period. I was more than thrilled to

cross. I intended to cross, but my ancestors over another boundary caught my attention. They were talking in telepathy, which caught my attention. I was born profoundly deaf and had all hearing family members, all of which knew sign language! I could read or communicate with about twenty ancestors of mine and others through telepathic methods. It overwhelmed me. I could not believe how many people I could telepathize with simultaneously.[3]

God promises that one day the blind will see, the deaf will hear, our children and loved ones who have had hardship here on earth will run and laugh and talk—and it will all be worth it. It is comforting to ponder what Mother Teresa said: "In light of heaven, the worst suffering on earth, a life full of the most atrocious tortures on earth, will be seen to be no more serious than one night in an inconvenient hotel."[4]

Jesus gave us a glimpse of the kingdom of Heaven where all that is diseased, broken, and living contrary to God's perfect plan will finally find healing, health, and wholeness. That's what we have to look forward to in Heaven. But in the meantime, we can bring more and more of God's kingdom here on earth as we use our God-given gifts and abilities to minister to people in need— physically, emotionally, and spiritually.

Today, look for ways to be a healing agent to those who are hurting or in need. Direct them to the Master Healer, keeping your eyes on the wholeness they will one day experience in the life to come.

Prayer: *Jesus, I look forward to the day when every physical, emotional, and spiritual hardship will be banished forever. Until then, grant me the grace I need each day to face my own hardship and to be a healing agent for others.*

36

I have told you these things so that you will be filled with my joy. Yes, your joy will overflow!

John 15:11 NLT

The LORD directs the steps of the godly. He delights in every detail of their lives.

Psalm 37:23 NLT

SOME PEOPLE FIND IT HARD to imagine laughter in Heaven, or that God has a sense of humor. But think about it—God is the creator of laughter, the author of all joy, and the one who delights in us and cares about every detail of our lives. Leonard discovered this during his NDE:

> On the other side, communication is done via telepathy (thought transfer). I must tell you that God has a fantastic sense of humor; I never laughed so much in all my life! We laughed about the way I had so seriously reacted to an event. Life on earth is a big drama! It should not be taken too much in earnest![1]

George Ritchie discovered that even his silliest thoughts could not be hidden in Jesus's presence. After he thought about the insurance policy he had just taken out guaranteeing him money when he turned seventy, he realized the Lord had a sense of humor: "The brightness seemed to vibrate and shimmer with a kind of holy laughter—not at me and my silliness, not a mocking laughter, but a mirth that seemed to say that in spite of all error and tragedy, joy was more lasting still."[2]

Nineteen-year-old Terry, who had an NDE while giving birth, said:

> [I] was enveloped in a beautiful light of love and knew I was being held on the lap of Jesus like a child. It is a feeling of unconditional

love. . . . Jesus and I had an astounding conversation where he patiently answered all my questions. One I distinctly remember: I had recently completed a grueling course in calculus and had gotten all the final exam answers correct except one—I wanted to know the answer to that question. Jesus laughed and then gave me the answer, not in words but in a "knowing" that encompassed not just the element of the question, but a complete understanding of all relational aspects of the question. HE has a wonderful sense of humor and I distinctly got the feeling that HE enjoys us humans as a father enjoys watching the minor scrapes children get themselves into.[3]

Jesus's genuine smile and delight impacted Julie:

He gave me that smile that only Jesus can give, and I knew the answer without him having to say anything. We walked and talked for a while. . . . He knew and answered my thoughts and I didn't need to open my mouth. . . . I asked Jesus, "What do you do here in Heaven?" He looked at me with this humorous smile that is beyond explanation in human words.[4]

It is amazing to think how personal God is and how much joy he feels about his children. God finds pure delight in the thought of you and all you are created to be. You are his treasure, his work of art, just as you are. He loves how he designed you!

Jesus wants to enter into every detail of your life and fill you with his overflowing joy. Set your mind on God's delight in you and his guidance in your life. He sees the good in everything now and yet to come, and you can trust him. Today, focus on his warm and loving presence in your life, and imagine Jesus's big smile beaming with pleasure as you enjoy life with him.

Prayer: *Thank you, Jesus, for smiling upon me and taking delight in me. I want my life to be filled with your presence and to reflect your joy to others.*

37

For God, who said, "Let there be light in the darkness," has made this light shine in our hearts so we could know the glory of God that is seen in the face of Jesus Christ.

2 Corinthians 4:6 NLT

For once you were full of darkness, but now you have light from the Lord. So live as people of light!

Ephesians 5:8 NLT

THE HIGHLIGHT for many near-death experiencers is this God of light who fills them with a love beyond imagination. The characteristics they report of this God of light are amazingly consistent with what the Old Testament prophets and Jesus revealed.

Captain Dale Black recalls:

The closer I got to the city [of God], the more distinct the illumination became. The magnificent light I was experiencing emanated from about forty or fifty miles within the city wall. I saw a great phosphorescent display of light that narrowed to a focal point that was brighter than the sun. Oddly, it didn't make me squint to look at it. And all I wanted to do was to look at it.

The light was palpable. It had substance to it, weight and thickness, like nothing I had ever seen before or since. The light from a hydrogen bomb is the closest I can come to describing it. Just after the bomb is detonated—but before the fireball that forms the mushroom cloud—there is a millisecond of light that flashes as the bomb releases its energy. It was something like that but much larger. . . .

Somehow I knew that light and life and love were connected and interrelated. It was as if the very heart of God lay open for everyone in heaven to bask in its glory, to warm themselves in its presence, to bathe in its almost liquid properties so they could be restored, renewed, refreshed. Remarkably, the light didn't shine on things but through them. Through the grass. Through the trees. Through the wall. And through the people who were gathered there.[1]

Researcher Steve Miller interviewed another NDEr who reported the same light, love, and personality of God:

> [The light] was of a kind that I'd never seen before and that differs from any other kind such as sunlight. It was white and extremely bright, and yet you could easily look at it. It's the pinnacle of everything there is. Of energy, of love especially, of warmth, of beauty. I was immersed in a feeling of total love.
>
> . . . From the moment the light spoke to me, I felt really good—secure and loved. The love which came from it is just unimaginable, indescribable. It was a fun person to be with! And it had a sense of humor, too—definitely! I never wanted to leave the presence of this being.[2]

Jesus is the light of the world! His light displaces the darkness, illuminating God's love, and we have access to its transformational power to fill our hearts to shine brightly for Him.

As God fills Heaven with his presence and light, he also will fill us now, and he desires to meet our deepest longings here on earth. God wants to enter into our lives and shine his light on all of our darkness, replacing it all with the love and life that only he can give.

God promises that you will share in his glory in Heaven one day (Col. 3:4). Imagine experiencing this for eternity. In gratitude, let it motivate you to be a light shining in the darkness, full of God's love and infused with his zeal for life today.

Prayer: *Dear God, thank you that you are the light, life, and love this world desperately needs. Shine your light into all areas of my life, so I can reflect your love and be life-giving to those around me today.*

38

Holy Father, protect them by the power of your name, the
name you gave me, so that they may be one as we are one.
While I was with them, I protected them and kept them safe
by that name you gave me.

John 17:11–12

SEVENTEEN-YEAR-OLD TRAVON discovered the power of Jesus's name when his car skidded out of control.

As soon as my car struck the pole, I saw nothing. Immediately, I
presumed that I was dead, but soon realized that I was still conscious
and this shouldn't be. . . .

Quietly at first, I began hearing non-worldly voices and screams
of evil or laughter. I became scared and didn't know what was
going on. The voices got louder and louder and soon, I could "feel"
the presence of beings or evil all around me. The voices began to
become more distinctive and some of the "beings" were shouting
"Come with us, come with us! . . . Are you ready for it?!" in very
scary voice tones. I began to realize that it sounded as though these
were demons or evil beings associated with Satan.

Even though before the experience I was very critical of religion
and God, these things were convincing me otherwise, and I immediately began saying, "Jesus loves me!!! The power of God will
kill you all. Jesus, save me!!" The beings started to yell, furious . . .
so I continued, "Jesus, save me!! I believe in you, Jesus, God help
me!" And the demons continued to yell and curse at me, but at the
same time they were slowly retracting. . . .

At this moment a piercing white beam of light the width of a
pen shot down to us. The demons began screaming and moaning,
as if they were melting and soon they disappeared. The light was
literally blinding, but I could stare directly into it without flinching.
. . . I felt this enormous presence of love and respect and everything
good. . . . The light was getting brighter at this time, and wider.

Soon, Jesus appeared in front of me, and I could do nothing but fall to my knees and then lay my head on the floor at his feet. It was like that for an eternity, and then Jesus said, "You are worthy child, rise." So I did and faced the Lord Jesus Christ. . . . Jesus said, "You have learned from your mistakes, my child. You will return, and you will show others the way. You will spread the love of God."

I immediately began to weep uncontrollably (yes, even though I'm a seventeen-year-old dude) and kept saying, "I am unworthy, Lord." At this moment, I was in the presence of my deceased relatives, two uncles, an aunt, a grandfather and a great-grandmother of whom none spoke but they pointed to the "ground," indicating I must return. At this point, I was spontaneously in my mortal body in the hospital looking up at my parents and friends.[1]

We live in a world where spiritual forces continually try to lie to us, attempting to discourage and distract us from living the life God desires for his beloved. In Christ, we have been given authority to stand against these forces in the name of Jesus.

As a believer, you do not need to fear evil, for it has no power over you. The only power it has is what you allow. Reject and resist any voices you hear in your mind that are not in the character of God. Voices of condemnation, hopelessness, hatred of self or others, rejection, despair, accusation—when these thoughts come, stand against them! Replace them by calling out God's truths of mercy, grace, acceptance, hope, unconditional love, kindness, and a positive future he sees for you.

"Fix your thoughts on what is true, and honorable, and right, and pure, and lovely, and admirable. Think about things that are excellent and worthy of praise"(Phil. 4:8–9 NLT). Today, speak the powerful name of Jesus and the truths of Scripture over your fears and negative thoughts, and feel your heart and spirit lift with his presence.

Prayer: *Jesus, there is great power in your name! Help me to speak it over the lies that distract me from living in your love and truth about me.*

39

> Do not let your heart be troubled; believe in God, believe also in Me. In My Father's house are many dwelling places; if it were not so, I would have told you; for I go to prepare a place for you.
>
> John 14:1–2 NASB

IN HEAVEN, Jesus had a surprise to show Hannah before she returned to earth:

Jesus wanted me to go with Him somewhere and He wanted to show me a few things. I walked with Him for what seemed like a very long while. The landscaping was so perfect and everything was in bloom. It was such a magical place beyond words.

I remember walking on this path/street with Jesus and we came to a house, or part of one, anyway. I could see the side of the house had a body of water. Jesus said it was a reflection pond. I was eager to check it out and went ahead of Jesus to get a better look. I turned around to see where Jesus was and He was just watching me in all my excitement: eyes wide and full of Love for me, still smiling as big as can be. I waited for Him to come closer to me and He told me, "This is your house." I said, "Really, this is my house?" It was perfect, and I loved it without even seeing it.

We went into the house and I wanted to go right out to the reflection pond. . . . I just couldn't believe the house was mine; it was perfect.[1]

Gary's friend John showed him his house, which was still under construction:

John then led me through gates that sparkled of precious stones. Up the walkway stood the mansion where I will spend all eternity. It had great, marble columns, like some of the plantations you see in the South. It was magnificent.

Walking into the mansion, we entered into what would be like a living room area. There was no furniture, only three buckets of paint sitting there. I had seen other mansions that had furniture, art on the walls, some even had pets—all the trappings of suburbia that we have here on earth. No two mansions were alike; God knows you better than you know yourself. He knows your heart's desires, your likes and dislikes. . . .

"This place needs more decorating," he said. . . . Suddenly, there was this beautiful, floral garden and scenery that was manifested before my eyes. A beautiful fragrance, like roses, consumed the room. I stood there gazing at the splendor of it all, thinking, "Could this be all for me?" Could the answer be as simple as "Yes, because Jesus loves me"? John looked at me and said, "It's not ready for occupancy just yet."[2]

How delightful to imagine our dream home for eternity. And to think of such beauty surrounding us, with nothing run-down or broken or in need of repair—too good to be true!

Jesus has promised a beautiful, peaceful, secure home in Heaven for all those who choose to live for him here on earth. No need to "keep up with the Joneses" when you have a dream home designed in Heaven to live in for all eternity. This can help you to be grateful and content with the home you have, even as you look forward to the home that awaits you. Don't worry, it will meet all your expectations and more, for God knows the desires of your heart.

Today, when you feel pressure to compare your home or material possessions to those of others, set your mind on your eternal dwelling. Live for what truly matters. You will be rewarded in Heaven for prioritizing the important things while on earth.

Prayer: *Dear Lord, thank you for such a wonderful home to live in one day! Help me to be content with what I have now and to prioritize what is most on your heart during my short time on earth.*

40

Have mercy on me, O God, according to your unfailing love; according to your great compassion blot out my transgressions. . . . [W]ash me, and I will be whiter than snow. Let me hear joy and gladness.

Psalm 51:1, 7–8

A YOUNG SINGLE WOMAN from England experienced the compassion of the Savior after attempting to abort her baby alone and in secret, resulting in her own near death as well:

Suddenly the pain stopped. I felt calm for the first time in 3 months since learning of my pregnancy by a man who had lied to me, telling me he loved me and wanted to marry me, but who had a wife and 5 children in another city. I had a very clear view of my body as they ferociously worked on me. . . .

[I] floated into a place which was overwhelmed by a radiant white light that seemed to embody all the concepts of love. A love which was unconditional, and like a mother has for a child . . . a warm joyful presence. . . . I knew in my heart that this was God. Words can't describe my awe in this presence. At that time, I recall wondering if I would be punished for murdering my child and in doing so, kill[ing] myself as well. I could tell He knew my every thought and feeling. . . .

I watched [the Life Review] with fascination as I saw the highlights of each stage of my life. . . . I watched and felt my mother's shame as she bore me out of wedlock right up to the elation of love and the crushing pain of rejection and betrayal. I understood the fear and insecurities of the man that caused my pain, and his own guilt upon breaking up with me upon learning of my pregnancy. I felt every good or bad deed I had ever done and [its] consequences upon others. It was a difficult time for me, but I was supported by unconditional love and weathered the painful parts. . . .

He showed me a beautiful shiny bubble which floated next to me. In it I saw a tiny baby nursing at a breast. The baby became a toddler and began walking toward me. . . . Then the image of a young boy turned into a teenager, and he continued to age until he was a full grown man. "Who is that?" I asked. "Your son, Michael," was the reply. I recall feeling very relieved that I hadn't destroyed his chance at life.

A flood of fearful thoughts crowded into my mind. I wasn't even married and could barely support myself, how could I raise a son? I saw a flash of myself with a man I knew to be my future husband, and he was holding the 2-year-old boy I saw in the picture. For the first time, I allowed myself to feel love for the baby I was carrying. All the embarrassment, complications and hardships I had used to rationalize my abortion seemed very weak and selfish.

Suddenly, I was popped back into my body and searing pain tore through [me]. . . . My doctor said it was a miracle that he was able to save the baby along with myself. . . . I went ahead with my life optimistically, with a whole new attitude, and delivered a healthy baby boy 5 months later, and I named him Michael.[1]

No matter what you have done in your past or what you are struggling with today, you have always been deeply loved by your Heavenly Father and always will be. He sees who you are meant to be, and who you can become!

In Psalm 51, after he committed adultery with Bathsheba and had her husband killed to cover up his sin, King David leaned on God's mercy and compassion. If you are feeling condemned or trapped like there is no way out, you can be set free. Jesus paid for it all on the cross so you don't have to pay for it anymore. Fully trust him—he will forgive you and help you overcome.

In this moment, release all your cares to him, and let his Spirit fill you with his presence and peace to face whatever comes. God is compassionate and gracious; you can trust him with your burdens and mistakes.

Prayer: *Father, thank you for the cleansing power of your forgiveness and your unfailing love for me. Guide me forward into the life you created me to live.*

41

Then the righteous will shine like the sun in the kingdom of their Father. Whoever has ears, let them hear.

Matthew 13:43

JESUS TEACHES THAT WE WILL REFLECT God's glory in Heaven. It is fascinating that thousands around the world who have these near-death experiences report seeing people in Heaven who can appear as we know them now, or who can shine with an extraordinary brightness, radiating a light that comes from within. Those who see Jesus say he shines the most brilliant of all.

When Vicki, a blind woman, was asked if there was a certain brightness associated with Jesus, she responded, "Much more than anybody there. He was the brightest of anybody there at all . . . but it was incredibly beautiful and warm. It was very intense. I know I couldn't have stood it if I were myself ordinarily."[1]

Dr. Mary Neal talked candidly about the people she saw. She was reluctant to give them a name, since they shined with this unearthly glory:

They had heads, arms, legs. They were wearing robes of a sort, but they were absolutely exploding with a pure, pure love. . . . A brilliance of light, just exploding in it and the light was not just something you would see. If you look at the sun, you see light and it's blinding. This was really a light born out of love. I don't know quite how else to explain it but it was brilliant and overpowering. I mean, it permeated everything, and I could be with them, and I knew without any doubt that I had known them and loved them as long as I've existed. I knew that they knew me and loved me as long as I existed.[2]

That must be what Paul meant when he encouraged us to become "'children of God without fault in a warped and crooked generation.' Then you will shine among them like stars in the sky. . . . [And he] will transform our lowly bodies so that they will be like his glorious body" (Phil. 2:15; 3:21).

You were created to share in God's glory—the very life, love, and light of God filling your being. Don't settle by living for anything less when you can radiate God's image. His joy is incomparable to anything this world could offer!

The world pushes us to find our worth in things that will never fully satisfy. God never intended for you to base your identity on anything other than God—not on accomplishments or performances, not on what others say about you, not on any material wealth or status you could achieve.

Look what God says about your true identity: "Bring my sons from afar and my daughters from the ends of the earth—everyone who is called by my name, whom I created for my glory, whom I formed and made" (Isa. 43:6–7). God made you for himself—not to prove your glory, but to be his glory and shine his love. As his children, we have the light of God within us to radiate his love out into the world!

Today, fully embrace the fact that your identity is found only in God. He is fully pleased with what he has made! Open your heart to be filled with his glory so he can shine through you, and you can radiate the best version of you to the world.

Prayer: *Lord Jesus, I am honored to one day share in your glory. Today, let me radiate your love as you shine through me to those I encounter.*

42

And we know that God causes everything to work together for the good of those who love God and are called according to his purpose for them.

Romans 8:28 NLT

HOWARD STORM RECALLS that during his NDE Jesus and the angels told him God not only knows everything that will come to pass in the future, but also, more importantly, God knows everything that could happen.

> He is aware of every possible variation and every possible outcome. God gives each of us free will—he won't violate our free will or dictate the outcome of everything—yet at the same time, the outcome will always serve God's purpose in the end, no matter how long it takes to unfold or how impossible it might seem.[1]

During his NDE, Dr. Alexander felt he understood the reason suffering and evil exist.

> Without free will, evil is impossible, he explains. But without free will, humans cannot grow or move forward. Without free will, there is no opportunity for us to grow into what God yearns for us to be. The Creator allows evil to exist as a necessary consequence of the gift of free will.[2]

God promises to overcome evil one willing heart at a time. And when we turn back to him, he will even make something good of all our suffering, as Scripture promises:

> Yet what we suffer now is nothing compared to the glory he will reveal to us later. For all creation is waiting eagerly for that future day when God will reveal who his children really are. Against its will, all creation was subjected to God's curse. But with eager

hope, the creation looks forward to the day when it will join God's children in glorious freedom from death and decay. For we know that all creation has been groaning as in the pains of childbirth right up to the present time. . . . God causes everything to work together for the good of those who love God and are called according to his purpose for them. (Rom. 8:18–22, 28 NLT)

Freedom is risky because free-willed creatures who turn from God and thwart his love hurt each other. But love that is not free to choose is not love at all. Love cannot be forced. Yet still, God will make something good out of the brokenness.

God promises to wipe away every tear. All pain and suffering will cease in Heaven, and we will see then how he used it all for our good. He wants us to have confidence in this promise, so that we won't turn from him when we suffer at the hands of a world that has chosen to exist apart from God's will and ways.

Today, hold on to the hope that everything will ultimately count for your good when you stand on the promises of God by faith. Confidently own the victory that is yours through Christ, and choose to cling to God in the midst of whatever the world brings your way. You are called for God's purposes, and he will make something beautiful out of all your experiences, no matter what.

Prayer: *Lord, thank you for allowing me to love you freely and choose to serve you willingly. Please help me to hold on to the hope that you can make something good out of every situation.*

43

You will have to live with the consequences of everything you say. What you say can preserve life or destroy it; so you must accept the consequences of your words.

Proverbs 18:20–21 GNT

RENE WAS DRIVING HOME in Sydney, Australia, when her car crashed. She was pronounced dead by the neurosurgeon at the hospital. But she was very much alive:

I arrived in an explosion of glorious light into a room with insubstantial walls, standing before a man about in his 30's about 6 foot tall, reddish brown shoulder length hair and an incredibly neat, short beard & moustache. He wore a simple white robe, light seemed to emanate from Him and I felt He had great age and wisdom. He welcomed me with great Love, Tranquility, Peace (indescribable), no words. I felt "I can sit at your feet forever and be content," which struck me as a strange thing to think/say/feel.

He stood beside me and directed me to look to my left, where I was replaying my life's less complimentary moments; I relived those moments and felt not only what I had done but also the hurt I had caused. Some of the things I would have never imagined could have caused pain. I was surprised that some things I may have worried about, like shoplifting a chocolate as a child, were not there, whilst casual remarks which caused hurt unknown to me at the time were counted. When I became burdened with guilt I was directed to other events which gave joy to others.[1]

Our words matter to God. Howard Storm realized firsthand the severity of using God's name flippantly:

How many times in my life had I denied and scoffed at the reality before me? How many thousands of times had I used the name of God as a curse? What incredible arrogance to use the name of God as an insult. Such a travesty against all that is holy. I was terribly ashamed to go closer. The wonderful, incredible intensity of the emanations of goodness and love might be more than I could bear. . . . During my home life and later as an art student, I had acquired the habit of swearing profusely. This became an unconscious habit and meant nothing to me. To use vulgar words is only poor taste. To use the name of God in crude or empty ways is an insult to our Creator. I was horrified at how it hurt my heavenly company when we witnessed me blaspheming God and Christ Jesus in my life review.[2]

Our words have the power to give life, and they have the power to destroy life. Too often we say things without thinking, causing harm to our children, family, and friends. Sometimes we intentionally use our words to take a jab at someone, just to make ourselves feel better. But this is not the character of God.

God is love; he is kindness; he encourages and builds up. And we have the privilege every day to represent him by speaking love and encouragement to others. Our words should be chosen wisely and used to build up and affirm others whenever we have the chance. This is true even when we give tough love to those who need it. Truth should never be given in harsh or arrogant ways. Instead, we are to be healing agents. Proverbs 12:18 says, "The words of the reckless pierce like swords, but the tongue of the wise brings healing."

Our words can also hurt God. When God's holy name is used in vain and careless ways, especially by believers who know him, this is serious to God. The third of the Ten Commandments says, "You shall not misuse the name of the LORD your God, for the LORD will not hold anyone guiltless who misuses his name" (Exod. 20:7). Today, thoughtfully choose words that will affirm and bless the people in your life, including God, as you respect his holy name. In doing this, you will not only be an encouragement to others but an instrument of healing in their lives.

Prayer: *Dear God, help me speak affirming words to bless and lift up others, and to give utmost respect to your holy name in my speech throughout the day.*

44

Speak the truth in love, growing in every way more and more like Christ, who is the head of his body, the church.

Ephesians 4:15 NLT

DIANA HAD BEEN THROUGH a very tough life. During her NDE, she felt a purity of communication she'd never experienced before:

We began to communicate when I understood [God] was "speaking" to me. . . . It was not with spoken words but more like with complete thoughts with no possibility of misunderstanding. It was a true communication of perfect understanding between two spirits. I would "ask," then would "know" the answer from the golden, glowing, loving being. . . .

I reveled in that complete, pure communication. There was no possibility of misunderstandings or evasions. There were no words to confuse the issue, only the truth of learning and knowing each other between us. This is how we were supposed to communicate and understand between two people. It's that "heart to heart" talk taken to the ultimate level.

I feel the lack of it here. Words are so bulky and awkward compared to just "showing" you how I feel or what I think. In every sentence I write here, I feel the weight and awkwardness of these words.[1]

Dean shares a similar discovery he found during his NDE:

Because everything is alive, everything can communicate so that you "experience" the communication—you don't just hear it. There was no miscommunication, no misunderstandings. There was nothing you would hide from one another . . . every thought was pure. There was a rule that you did not go into any other's thoughts without them giving you permission to do so.[2]

Crystal likens this perfect communication to having a password that allows instant access to another's innermost thoughts, allowing a more complete understanding and connection than could ever be possible on earth. She says, "There was no room whatsoever for secrets or shame or misunderstanding or anything negative. There was just this wonderful, beautiful, nourishing sense of knowing."[3]

In Heaven's perfect place, we will be free of the myriad of problems that misunderstandings and miscommunications cause. In addition, all the deceptions of lying, hiding, and covering the truth will be left behind. This will feel so liberating! Communication will be like what Jesus described: "There is nothing concealed that will not be disclosed, or hidden that will not be made known" (Matt. 10:26).

The integrity and honesty in Heaven is expected of us now in this life as well. This is living in God's truth and light (1 John 1:5–7), and it is how he will accomplish his will through us relationally. In situations where it is tempting to stretch the truth to make yourself look better, tell a "white lie" to your kids, or avoid representing yourself truthfully in order to dodge an awkward situation, be honest, even if it requires humility. This honors God, and he will reward you for bringing Heaven's ways of communicating to earth.

Let this be your goal today—seek to truly listen and understand the heart and mind of others, and commit to being upright and fully honest in all your communications.

Prayer: *Father, I look forward to the day when communication will be clear, direct, and true. Help me today to grow in my integrity and honesty, seeking to understand others in all my interactions.*

45

I have filled him with the Spirit of God . . . and with all kinds
of skills—to make artistic designs.

Exodus 31:3–4

There are different kinds of gifts, but the same Spirit distrib-
utes them . . . in all of them and in everyone it is the same
God at work.

1 Corinthians 12:4–6

TODAY I MET GOD," whispered four-year-old Akiane to
her mother.

"What is God?" asked her mother, Foreli, who was
raised as an atheist in Lithuania.

"God is light—warm and good. It knows everything and talks
with me. It is my parent."

The family had never talked religion, never gone to church, they
didn't even own a TV, and so this shocked Foreli.

About the same time Akiane claimed to have visits with God,
she began to draw. But her drawings at age four and five surpassed
high school–level art students—seeming miraculous. After draw-
ing "her angel," she explained, "You see, where God takes me, He
teaches me how to draw."

Akiane claimed God took her to Heaven where she saw a "house
of light with walls like glass" where God lives, a place of beautiful
grass, trees, plants, and fruit. "I am good there, and I listen there,"
explained Akiane. "Everyone listens there—God is there. . . . The
music there is alive."

Akiane's talk of God the Father, Jesus, and the Holy Spirit com-
bined with her supernatural gift for art eventually led her family
to faith. As Akiane grew, her amazing artistic abilities expanded

from drawings to paintings, and at age seven she began composing shockingly mature, spiritual poems, far beyond her years.

By age eight, Akiane's paintings of Jesus were gaining world-wide recognition. She claimed to see Jesus in Heaven and painted the renowned works "The Prince of Peace" and "Father Forgive Them" as a result. Every major news program in America and many around the world began to recognize her as the only binary child prodigy alive (for art and poetry). She says the purpose of her art is "to draw people's attention to God, and I want my poetry to keep their attention on God."

Around age ten, Akiane was asked why she had decided on Christianity rather than a different world religion. "I didn't choose Christianity," Akiane replied. "I chose Jesus Christ. I am painting and writing what God shows me."[1]

God gives all of his children gifts. In 1 Corinthians 12, the apostle Paul lists some of the various gifts, services, and ministries God empowers each of us by his Spirit to do. Every one of us has been given special gifts and abilities to build up others.

We can choose to use out gifts to build our own kingdom, or we can use them to build God's kingdom. Whatever they are—encouragement, teaching, leading, creativity, music, hospitality, wisdom, compassion—there are numerous ways to use our gifts to serve God and people.

If you are not sure what your gifts are, ask God to show you. You also might ask people close to you how they see God naturally using you to build up others. As Paul said in 2 Timothy 1:6, God gives the gifts, but we still have to develop them. Think about how you might develop and exercise your spiritual gifts today.

> **Prayer:** *God, thank you for giving me gifts not just for my benefit, but to build up your body, the church, and to point people to you. Show me how I can develop the gifts you've given me.*

46

But now that he is dead, why should I go on fasting? Can I bring him back again? I will go to him, but he will not return to me.

2 Samuel 12:23

J EFF FELT INTENSE DESPAIR over losing his wife and baby Griffin in a car accident. He struggled to let them go, wanting to die and be with them, yet knowing he needed strength to stay and father four-year-old Spencer who survived along with him. At a crisis point during his recovery, he had another near-death experience of Heaven.

As I walked, on two healthy strong legs, I entered into a long hallway . . . and at the end of the hallway was a baby crib. I rushed to the crib, and peeking in, saw something beyond joyful. There lying in the crib was my son. It was little Griffin! He was alive and well. He slept so peacefully. I looked at him and took in every detail. How his chubby little hands lay so peacefully beside his perfect face . . . how his hair lay gently across the tops of his ears.

I reached into the crib and swept him up into my arms. I could feel the warmth from his little body. I could feel his breath on my neck and the smell of his delicate hair. He was so familiar and so alive! . . . I held him close and cried tears of joy as I laid my cheek against his soft little head as we had always done. . . . It was Griffin! He was alive, and I was with him, holding him in this wonderful place. . . .

I felt something or someone move up behind me. The feeling coming from this being was so powerful and yet so loving that it almost startled me. I felt light and love engulf me. . . . I knew my wife and son were gone. They had died months earlier, but time didn't exist where I was at that moment.

Rather than having them ripped away from me, I was being given the opportunity to actually hand them over to God. To let them go in peace, love, and gratitude. Everything suddenly made sense. Everything had divine order. I could give my son to God and not have him taken away from me. . . .

I held my baby son as God himself held me. I experienced the oneness of all of it . . . the being behind me inviting me to let it all go and give Griffin to Him. In all that peace and knowledge, I hugged my little boy tightly one last time, kissed him on the cheek, and gently laid him back down in the crib. I willingly gave him up. No one would ever take him away from me again. He was mine. We were one, and I was one with God. . . . Griffin was alive in a place more real than anything here.[1]

The greatest love we feel for children, a spouse, friends, or family on earth amounts to a teaspoon of love compared to the oceans we will experience together for eternity. God is love, and Heaven will be the greatest reunion ever! When King David's infant son died, 2 Samuel says David declared his hope that even though his son could not come back to him, he would one day go to be with his son.

Maybe you, too, are grieving the loss of a child or someone else very close to your heart. Even though it may seem difficult, in your sorrow draw near to God. He loves you, and you can trust your loved ones into his care. Find comfort in knowing that your Father in Heaven loves them more than you could ever imagine.

Today, allow the peace and comfort of God to fill your heart with assurance that your loved ones are in God's care. This hope can empower you to move forward positively in your life. Like King David, have confidence you will see your loved ones again and experience the joy of being together and loving them forever.

> **Prayer:** *Father, I hope for the day to reunite with my loved ones who have gone to Heaven before me. I place them in your hands. Help me to live today fully, even without them, knowing that joy is coming when I will be with them again forever.*

47

See what great love the Father has lavished on us, that we should be called children of God! And that is what we are!

1 John 3:1

But I am like an olive tree flourishing in the house of God; I trust in God's unfailing love forever and ever.

Psalm 52:8

DEAN BRAXTON'S HEART STOPPED for an hour and forty-five minutes during kidney surgery. He revived, claiming he saw Jesus and had a wonderful experience of Heaven's Love:

When I first arrived in Heaven and knelt before Jesus, all I could do was say, "You did this for me? Thank You! Thank You, thank You!" Everything in me cried out in praise to Jesus. It was pure joy. . . .

His love is alive. It is more than just a sense. You are becoming His love. You are His love. Jesus loves us completely. . . . It was like I was the only one He loved in all of His creation.

God the Father [was] singing back to each and every being giving Him praise before the Throne. . . . That is what was going on in Heaven. Father God was expressing His love for each being and they were expressing their love for Him.[1]

Dr. Mary Neal summarizes how difficult it is to try to adequately describe the purity of Love that is felt in Heaven:

One of the problems that I and most people had when they came back from a near-death experience is that even the most intense beauty here on Earth, even the most intense love here on Earth, is very, very pale in comparison to the intensity of the love and to the intensity of the beauty in God's world, when everything was imbibed with an absolute and pure love . . . love of God.[2]

God loves you more than you can imagine! You are his child. The incredible love you feel for your children, spouse, or other people in your life can't even come close to the breadth and depth of the love God has for you. And he knows you more intimately than anyone else ever could.

He loves you just the way you are. No other person can have the unique relationship with God that he created you to have with him. His love for you is unwavering and will never change.

> And I am convinced that nothing can ever separate us from God's love. Neither death nor life, neither angels nor demons, neither our fears for today nor our worries about tomorrow—not even the powers of hell can separate us from God's love. No power in the sky above or in the earth below—indeed, nothing in all creation will ever be able to separate us from the love of God that is revealed in Christ Jesus our Lord. (Rom. 8:38–39 NLT)

Imagine in Heaven when you fully comprehend how special you are to the most important Being in the universe! Today, set your mind on how God feels about you, and how much he loves and adores you. Because you are in Christ, you can live confidently out of his unchanging security.

Prayer: *Heavenly Father, thank you for lavishing upon me such pure love. Help me to live filled up with your love every moment of every day.*

48

Jesus stood and said in a loud voice, "Let anyone who is thirsty come to me and drink. Whoever believes in me, as Scripture has said, rivers of living water will flow from within them." By this he meant the Spirit, whom those who believed in him were later to receive.

John 7:37–39

GARY, WHO "DIED" IN A CAR ACCIDENT, was greeted by his best friend, John, who took him on a tour of the City of God:

We left the library, and I was taken to a grand auditorium. Everyone was clothed in glowing robes, and as I entered into the arena, I found I was clothed in a robe also.

Looking up, I saw a beautiful, spiral staircase winding up loftily into the heights of the atmosphere [like in Solomon's temple; see 1 Kings 6:8]. A beautiful, crystal clear river of water flowed directly in front of me. My eyes followed the river that flowed from the throne of God! It was an awesome sight to see the source of the river that was the throne of almighty God! . . .

Growing along the crystal river were orchards of fruit-bearing trees. . . . The hills and mountains before us towered in breathtaking beauty.

John told me to drink of the water. Tasting the water, I found it to be very sweet. John then guided me into the water. Stepping in, I discovered it was only ankle deep, and then it began to rise. It covered my thighs and my shoulders, until my entire being was eventually submerged. . . .

The beautiful water was actually cleansing me of any debris that may have clung to me in my transition from earth to glory. In the water, John and I could communicate with one another without verbally expressing ourselves. . . . The water receded, and we came out on the other side of the bank.[1]

Another NDEr shared similar discoveries:

> As we walked into the river, it got deeper and deeper until finally the surface of the river was over the top of our head[s], we were still breathing and so then I got the understanding, this is the flowing of the Spirit of God; it is a manifestation of the Spirit of God.[2]

Imagine plunging into the River of Life in Heaven, with characteristics of living water unlike any water you've experienced. Jesus offered living water to anyone who is thirsty. We have access to his living water even now on earth, as God's Spirit dwells within us and is alive and at work in our lives.

Too often we forget about the wonderful inner strength we have available to us through the Holy Spirit. He gives us what we need to be more like Jesus: "The Holy Spirit produces this kind of fruit in our lives: love, joy, peace, patience, kindness, goodness, faithfulness, gentleness, and self-control" (Gal. 5:22–23 NLT).

So go ahead and drink generously from the living water of his Holy Spirit, and these virtues will become more and more natural in your life. Your joy will increase, even during tough times. You will find peace replacing worry. You will find patience, love, and kindness in your heart where frustration and impatience once ruled. Drink deeply today.

> **Prayer:** *Heavenly Father, thank you for the gift of the Holy Spirit and for filling me with your presence and power. I want to drink freely of your living water, for it alone will satisfy my life's thirst and help me become more like you.*

49

Then the angel showed me the river of the water of life, as clear as crystal, flowing from the throne of God.

Revelation 22:1

For the Lamb on the throne will be their Shepherd. He will lead them to springs of life-giving water.

Revelation 7:17 NLT

REBECCA SPRINGER, who had an NDE in 1898, surprisingly writes of the same cleansing properties of the living water of Heaven as previously mentioned. When her deceased brother-in-law, Frank, took her in the river, she discovered:

> To my surprise and delight, I found I could not only breathe, but laugh and talk, see and hear, as naturally under the water as above it. I sat down in the midst of the many-colored pebbles, and filled my hands with them, as a child would have done. My brother lay down upon them . . . and laughed and talked joyously with me.
>
> "Do this," he said, rubbing his hands over his face, and running his fingers through his dark hair. I did as he told me, and the sensation was delightful. . . . As we neared the shore and my head once more emerged from the water, the moment the air struck my face and hair I realized that I would need no towel or brush. My flesh, my hair, and even my beautiful garments, were soft and dry as before the water touched them. . . .
>
> I turned and looked back at the shining river flowing on tranquilly. "Frank, what has that water done for me?" I said. "I feel as though I could fly." He looked at me with earnest, tender eyes, as he answered gently, "It has washed away the last of the earthlife, and fitted you for the new life upon which you have entered."
>
> "It is divine!" I whispered.
>
> "Yes, it is divine," he said.[1]

When an angel directed Ed Gaulden into the River of Life in Heaven, he discovered the same surprising qualities:

> "I can breathe!" I said, astonished. I spoke to the angel underwater, in clear tones without the words sounding bubbly.
>
> "You are standing in the River of Life. It is of the Spirit of God. It washes away the scars of sin. . . . You shall never thirst with this water. It flows from the Spirit of the Living God, feeding the Trees of Life."
>
> As we emerged from the River of Life, I noticed that I was not dripping wet![2]

Revelation 22:2 says the River of Life feeds the trees whose leaves are given for the healing of the nations. God will one day heal all of our scars from this life, and not just physical ones—our emotional and spiritual scars will also be made whole.

You don't have to wait to begin the process, because his Spirit, who is the Living Water, can cleanse you and fill you today. God has promised his Holy Spirit to every believer (see Eph. 1:13), and he will fill you with his abundant power and love as you remain connected to him.

Today, ask the Holy Spirit to show you the emotional or spiritual scars in your life that he is eager to begin healing now. Ask him how you can work with him in the healing process. Let Jesus lead you to springs of life-giving water, for his Spirit can meet every longing and heal every scar.

> **Prayer:** Lord, I thirst for a greater fullness of your Holy Spirit, and I long to be cleansed and healed of all the scars of this life. As I drink deeply of your living water, show me the areas in my life that need healing, and help me trust you fully.

50

I saw . . . someone like a son of man, dressed in a robe reaching down to his feet and with a golden sash around his chest. . . . [A]nd his eyes were like blazing fire.

Revelation 1:12–14

VICKI, WHO HAD BEEN BLIND FROM BIRTH, described Jesus's appearance and how she felt looking into his eyes during her NDE:

Interviewer: You saw a man whom you identified as Jesus. . . . Can you tell me what you remember being aware of when you saw Jesus? How he looked and so on?

Vicki: He embraced me, and I was very close to him. And I felt his beard and his hair. They were very close to me. He actually enveloped me—that's the only word I can think of to describe it. He enveloped me with so much warmth and love and with his actual physical presence. . . .

Interviewer: Did you see his eyes?

Vicki: They were piercing eyes. It was like they permeated every part of me, but . . . not in a mean way. It was like you couldn't lie about anything, and he just looked everywhere and he could see everything. Yet I wanted to reveal everything to him.

Interviewer: Was he wearing any kind of clothing?

Vicki: Yes. And his beard had very bright lights in it. . . . It was just light coming out of the beard itself. . . . There was nothing on his feet at all.

He had this kind of robe-thing on that didn't come all the way down to his feet. It was below the knees but above the ankles . . . then it had this sash around the waist part.[1]

Dean Braxton described the eyes of Jesus this way:

When I looked into Jesus' eyes, [they] were like flames of fire with changing colors of red, orange, blue, green, yellow, and many other colors. . . . I experienced in His eyes that they are deep and full of life. I could get lost in His eyes and never want to come out.[2]

Imagine how exhilarating it will be to look into the eyes of Jesus—breathtaking, blazing, all-knowing eyes of love. Eyes that will envelop you with peace and acceptance, surpassing anything you could ever imagine. Eyes that can pierce right through to your soul, yet with magnetic warmth that removes all fear as they draw you in.

Jesus sees everything, so there's no need to hide anything. He longs for you to look into his eyes and feel as loved as you are. He sees you as his beautiful and wonderful child—his beloved whom he wants to help be all God intended for you to be.

This moment, picture Jesus with his compassionate, loving eyes looking into yours. He wants to reassure you that you are completely and deeply loved.

Prayer: *Jesus, I long for the day when I will see you face-to-face and look into your loving eyes. Until that day, help me see myself the way you see me and find my identity completely in you alone.*

51

So be careful how you live. Don't live like fools, but like those who are wise. . . . Don't be drunk with wine, because that will ruin your life. Instead, be filled with the Holy Spirit.

Ephesians 5:15, 18 NLT

BEN HAD TURNED TO ALCOHOL to cope with life, and it ended up nearly killing him. He shares the lessons he learned from his NDE in hopes of helping others avoid what he did:

The beer, pot, and alcohol were flowing freely until around 2:00 am. I drank five to six bottles of beer along with two or three shots of whiskey. . . . All of a sudden, I experienced an intense pain across my chest. The last thing I remember before I left my body was falling backwards onto the floor. . . . I'd had a heart attack, died, and left my body behind.

All of a sudden, I was traveling through a tunnel at extreme speed. . . . Before I could adjust, I found myself in a very ornate light-filled room with a throne that was very high up. . . . I wanted desperately to hide from the presence of God, but there was no place to go to get away from his presence.

I was shown a review of my entire life, with joys, difficulties, sorrows, and everything in between. I saw myself being very kind to several people. I also heard unkind words I had spoken to others. I witnessed being ignored, and ignoring others. I was shown a love that had not worked out. I reviewed how others had abused me, which I didn't want to "see."

I really wasn't hearing words. It was more like telepathic communication, but there was no mistaking what was being communicated. God was not pleased by my life of alcohol and drugs. . . . I was shown a place of intense horror. I was not seeing with my eyes, but in some other way. Just before being consumed, I was guided away by a kindly person I knew to be Christ Jesus. . . . I found myself in the presence of many people that I "knew." I was surrounded by unconditional love, and, for lack of a better word, I was "home."

Then I was told to return to my life. . . . I must return and complete a prepared task, or work, that will change others. . . . [The] experience was definitely real.

As it concerns the trajectory of my life, I had been headed in the wrong direction—fast. Instead of being productive in society, I was thinking only of myself. I was bitter, hurt, and resentful. There were reasons for my negative feelings and thinking, but my life had no meaning or purpose. I was defeated and as good as dead. God shocked me into seeing beyond myself. Because of this experience, I have found that the only meaning in life is in how we love others in the present.[1]

It is clear that we live in a world that continuously tempts us to fill our bodies and minds with alcohol and other substances to "enjoy" life. Yet this is often how the evil one carries out his plan to lead us away from God's will when we are controlled by them.

It is common in our culture to self-medicate (especially condoned if the substances are "legal"). However, as salt and light in the world, we must put careful thought into our actions, since peer and cultural pressure will tempt us to manage our stress the wrong ways.

The good news is, God has given his Holy Spirit to fill us and guide us. The command in Ephesians 5:18 to "be filled with the Spirit" refers to a continual action ("keep on being filled"), not a one-time action. We must choose each moment to be filled with the Spirit's influence, just like choosing to be filled with a substance or not. The difference is, the Holy Spirit affects our minds in purely positive ways, leading us to do things that are loving, kind, and others-centered rather than regretful, careless, and self-centered.

Today and every day, choose to be led by the Holy Spirit instead of anything the world offers. You will feel the positive difference it makes in your life and circumstances.

Prayer: *Dear God, I want to be filled with your Spirit's love and power in my life and be guided only by you.*

52

He has made everything beautiful in its time. He has also
set eternity in the human heart.

Ecclesiastes 3:11

CAPTAIN DALE BLACK gives an amazing and detailed account
of his visit to the Heavenly City:

I was outside the city, slowly moving toward its wall, suspended
a few hundred feet above the ground. I'm not sure how I knew
directions there, but I had a strong, almost magnetic sense, that
it was northwest. Which meant I was approaching the city from
the southeast. A narrow road led to an entrance in the wall, which
led into the city. I moved effortlessly along the road, escorted by
my two angelic guides, on what seemed to be a divine schedule.

I was overwhelmed by its beauty. It was breathtaking. And a
strong sense of belonging filled my heart; I never wanted to leave.
Somehow I knew I was made for this place and this place was made
for me. . . . The entire city was bathed in light, an opaque white-
ness in which the light was intense but diffused. In that dazzling
light every color imaginable seemed to exist and—what's the right
word?—played. . . . It was breathtaking to watch. And I could have
spent forever doing just that. . . .

There was a huge gathering of angels and people, millions,
countless millions. They were gathered in a central area that seemed
over ten miles in diameter. The expanse of people was closer to an
ocean than a concert hall. Waves of people, moving in the light,
swaying to the music, worshiping God. . . . Somehow the music in
heaven calibrated everything, and I felt that nothing was rushed. . . .

The flowers in heaven fascinated me. Again, a delightful and
delicate balance between diversity and unity. Each was unique.
All were one. And they were beautiful to behold. Each petal and

leaf illuminated with that glorious light and added just the right splashes of color to the velvety expanse of green grass. . . .

The sky, the walls, the houses, everything was more beautiful than I ever dreamed anything could be. Even the colors. They were richer, deeper, more luminescent than any colors I have ever seen in the farthest reaches of earth or in the most fantastic of dreams. They were so vibrant they pulsated with life.[1]

As we imagine seeing and experiencing what Dale describes, it feels like a childhood fictional fantasy! Perhaps the reason we have the capacity to enjoy creating storybook fantasies here on earth is because of our innate longing for eternity and our desire to be in our real home.

This longing we feel has been given to us by God, for Scripture tells us "[God] has also set eternity in the human heart" (Eccles. 3:11). Like a bird's homing instinct, it's pointing us homeward, toward Heaven.

No matter what chaos or trials you must endure today, they are only temporary. Let this encourage and strengthen you as you persevere here on earth. You have an eternal home waiting for you—beautiful, pure, glorious, and governed by unconditional love.

You can look forward to this as you live out God's plan for your life now, confident he has a unique purpose for you to fulfill during your time on earth. So with expectant hope, set your mind on your true home and allow this to renew your perspective as you face the challenges today brings.

Prayer: *Father, as I face the day ahead, help me walk by faith and boldly trust you more. Thank you that I have an eternal home where love rules and all my longings will be satisfied.*

53

And he carried me away in the Spirit to a mountain great
and high, and showed me the Holy City, Jerusalem, coming
down out of heaven from God. It shone with the glory of
God, and its brilliance was like that of a very precious jewel,
like a jasper, clear as crystal. . . . The twelve gates were made
of pearls—each gate from a single pearl!

Revelation 21:10–11, 21

IMAGINE THE EXCITEMENT and anticipation that will well up
within you as you approach the gates and prepare to enter the
City of God. Brad Barrows, blind from birth, describes an
"immense field" stretching before him with huge palm trees and
tall grass as he approached the city:

> By this time, I was getting closer to the music and being abso-
> lutely fascinated by it. I wanted to join in with this music. It was
> absolutely precious. Within a very short amount of time . . . as I
> was going up the hill, I came to a large stone structure. I could tell
> that it was stone without even touching it. I could tell with some
> sort of sight that I had at that time, some sort of vision, I knew.
> They were almost like gem stones. They seemed to literally shine
> with their own particular light. Yet the light itself was actually
> penetrating right through the stones. It seemed that the stone was
> actually heightening that light, the light that was already there,
> to the point where I was almost afraid to touch those stones. I
> thought that they might be fiery hot. In another sense, I was very
> curious about them.
>
> The structure I was going into was a large tubular structure. I
> would say that at first the tube seemed to be at least a hundred feet
> in diameter, with the top of the tube being well over a hundred feet
> above my head. Right up to the tube, there were palm trees and
> grass, and again this large field that actually existed all the way up

to the entrance of this tube. When I got into the tubular structure itself, the ground suddenly changed, that is the consistency of the ground under me. When I looked into the tube, I could tell that I was going to step on some kind of stone, the same shiny, brilliant stone that I could see all around the tube. It was smooth stone, very, very smooth [like pearl!][1]

It's amazing that Brad, still blind today, vividly describes walking up the hilly meadows of Paradise, up to the gemstone foundation of the city wall shining with the glory of God, and into the archway of the city gate. He's describing what John described in Revelation 21!

What a thrill it must be for a blind person with newfound sight to see the City of God for the first time! In Heaven, every person will be complete and whole, lacking nothing. No matter what physical limitation you have now, what mental struggle, emotional challenge, or relational problem, you will be made perfect in your eternal home.

And the City of God will be like no other place you could ever imagine—constantly shining with the brilliant light, love, and glory of God. When you feel like you are in the darkness, set your mind on Heaven. Meditate on the wholeness you will experience in all things.

One day you will live in your real home—all the bad wiped away, only good things in store. Today, hold on to the hope that the struggles of this life cannot compare to the reward of Heaven awaiting you and the beauty you will experience forever.

Prayer: *Lord, nothing can compare to the perfect Heavenly city where you dwell. Thank you that you have prepared a place for me there. Help me to be faithful, knowing I will one day be where I truly belong—home!*

54

The body that is sown is perishable, it is raised imperishable; it is sown in dishonor, it is raised in glory; it is sown in weakness, it is raised in power; it is sown a natural body, it is raised a spiritual body.

1 Corinthians 15:42–44

GARY WOOD HAD A CAR ACCIDENT and was killed instantly. He recalls what happened after the impact:

I turned to see what the matter was. There was an explosion, then a sharp, instant pain seared across my face. There was a brilliant light that engulfed me, and I remember being free from all pain. I slipped out of my body. . . . I was above the car now. . . . As I began to ascend up through this tunnel of light, I felt such a tranquil feeling of peace wash over me. . . . All around me I could hear angels singing.

Gary found himself at the edge of an incredible city. As he entered, he discovered an unexpected reunion.

An angel nodded and I was granted access to the city. The first person I saw when I entered the city was my friend John who had been decapitated in an accident in high school. His death had been a haunting memory for me. When I saw him, I was overwhelmed with joy. He was just as I remembered him only so much more complete. He ran and embraced me. It was a glorious reunion. When he wrapped his arms around me, they went all the way through me—we went into one another. This hug was so much deeper than hugs on earth.

Gary revived twenty minutes after being pronounced "dead." Due to his injuries, he has no vocal cords. Yet he believes as a sign of what is to come, God did something the doctors still say is impossible. Gary says, "I have an X-ray that shows that I have no vocal cords, yet I talk and sing."[1]

When we die, we get an upgrade from our temporal, earthly bodies to a spiritual body that has a far greater "glory" and "power." How awesome it will feel to have a body like this for eternity!

Many of us may have lost loved ones who suffered physically, and it was heartbreaking to watch their once healthy bodies decline. It is comforting to know that in heaven, their bodies are healed, whole, and complete. Nothing is holding them back anymore. They are truly living life to the full!

If you or a loved one is currently experiencing earthly physical suffering, find comfort in the truth that one day in Heaven you will finally be free from the pain and hardship by which you feel constrained here on earth. There will come a day when your suffering will cease forever. You will experience healing and wholeness, with no limits to your abilities like you may have now—and that is a promise.

Remember, when you are weak, you are strong in Christ! He will do mighty things in and through you. Lean into his strength today, and let this give you courage to live the best life you can, even in your hardship.

> **Prayer:** *Dear Lord, I am grateful for my earthly body, even with the physical hardships that come, and I look forward to the day when I am whole and complete for eternity!*

55

For God so loved the world that he gave his one and only
Son, that whoever believes in him shall not perish but have
eternal life. For God did not send his Son into the world
to condemn the world, but to save the world through him.

John 3:16–17

DEAN BRAXTON WORKED as a psychologist counseling trau-
matized people. He said during his NDE,

> I had worked with children and teenagers over the past 33 years.
> During that time, the one issue that came up a lot with the children
> I had worked with was sexual abuse by adults. This one issue, to
> me, seems to do more damage than all the other issues I faced
> as a counselor. I have seen many people who had recovered from
> many types of abuse, but every time I had to deal with someone
> who had been sexually abused, the damage seemed to be the most
> harmful out of all the other abuses. I would always get upset on
> the inside of myself.

Feeling this astounding love Jesus had for every individual, Dean
asked Jesus thought to thought, "What about child molesters?"
since he felt sure that Jesus couldn't feel the same for them.

> Jesus said to me, "When you place a person in jail, they get out.
> They either get out when their time is up, or they get out when they
> die, but they get out . . . in hell, they are there for eternity." I also
> saw His arms outstretched like He was on the cross and He paid
> the price for everyone who sinned, or ever will sin, implying that
> we do not have a right to condemn anyone, since He does not. I
> knew that I knew—He wanted all people there with Him. He truly
> wants us there with Him. *All* people! But it is for each person to
> accept His atoning death for his or her sins in order to enter the
> newness of life He offers to us.[1]

Honestly, there's only one explanation that makes sense of a loving God allowing so much pain and suffering: he knows there's something much, much better or much, much worse ahead. He wants to save us all—the abused, the abuser, and everyone in between (see 1 Tim. 2:3).

It's not our nature to love with the kind of love God has, but through his strength and power we can love even our enemies. God wants all people to know his saving love and grace, and no one is beyond his loving reach.

When we pray for people who have harmed us or hurt others, we are participating in God's will for them to be redeemed and for evil to be overcome with good. God desires this for all people. Jesus said, "It is not my heavenly Father's will that even one of these little ones should perish" (Matt. 18:14 NLT).

God sees each person as his beloved child created to grow up into his image. Today, join with his heart and pray for opportunities to share the joy of your salvation with others who don't know him, so they too can be saved.

> **Prayer:** *Lord, I want to have your heart for others, and I don't want anyone to be without knowing you, including those hard-to-love people in my life. Please lead me to those with whom I can share your love and forgiveness today.*

56

I declare to you, brothers and sisters, that flesh and blood cannot inherit the kingdom of God, nor does the perishable inherit the imperishable. . . . For the perishable must clothe itself with the imperishable, and the mortal with immortality.

1 Corinthians 15:50, 53

WHAT AGE WILL WE BE IN HEAVEN? From some accounts, people appear to be all ages. As Gary Wood walked through the City of God with his best friend, John, he said, "I saw a playground with children and teenagers—those who died prematurely." At another point, he saw his grandmother and grandfather sitting on the front porch of a three-story house, talking to people walking by.[1]

Outside the city gate, Marv Besteman noticed a line of people who had just died, waiting to go inside:

Most of the men in line were between fifty and seventy years of age, and most of the women were between seventy and ninety years of age. There were three children in line, each of them around four or five years of age. These little ones were not standing still, but moving around, wiggling in their spots in line, like children do. They all had big smiles on their faces. Very soon I would see many, many babies in heaven . . . but while I was in line I noticed just one baby. He was of Indian heritage. . . . [A man] was carrying the tiny boy for . . . a young woman standing in front of him.[2]

He also saw his grandparents and noted:

Both of them were wearing clothing similar to what they wore on earth, and they appeared to be the age they were when they died. Still, Grandma and Grandpa looked like no other eighty-five-year-olds I have ever seen walking around here. I kid you not. Had I thrown a [football] pass at them, both of them gave the impression they could've easily jumped up and snatched it.[3]

Airline captain Dale Black noticed:

[I] saw them for who they were. None were skinny, none overweight. None were crippled, none were bent or broken. None were old, none were young. If I had to guess, I would say they appeared to be somewhere around thirty years old. . . . Although some form of time does seem to exist in heaven, no one aged.[4]

Another person shared:

Suddenly I recognized all these relatives. They were all around thirty-five years old, including the little brother I'd never known, because he had died during the war when he was two years old.[5]

Looking through the Scriptures, it is unclear what "age" we will be in Heaven. Doctors tell us our earthly bodies grow and develop until sometime in our late twenties or early thirties before we begin our slow decay, so perhaps that's our heavenly age.

Or perhaps we will be ageless, yet have the ability to appear to others as the age they knew us best. All this is theory, because Scripture seems silent on the topic, though it does tell us time in Heaven doesn't work like it does on earth.

Regardless, we will definitely be in our "prime" in the life to come! Knowing this, it is important to willingly embrace the stages of life here on earth as they unfold. Live fully in each age and stage, with the peace and joy God offers in every chapter of life.

Today, be mindful of how you are growing and maturing on the inside. Time and age will one day be irrelevant, but who you become on earth in the process will last.

Prayer: *Lord, thank you for the promise that my aging body will one day be ageless. In the meantime, please help me live with contentment, peace, and joy in every season of my life.*

57

His voice was like the sound of rushing waters. . . . His face was like the sun shining in all its brilliance.

Revelation 1:15–16

Today, if you hear his voice, do not harden your hearts.

Hebrews 3:7–8

GOD HAS A VOICE unlike any other. It's amazing how many NDErs describe the voice of God with the same words as the prophets. At times his voice is soft and loving, yet authoritative; other times it is unmistakably powerful and majestic.

The prophet Ezekiel said, "I saw the glory of the God of Israel coming from the east. His voice was like the roar of rushing waters" (Ezek. 43:2). The prophet Daniel saw the angel of God's presence and described a man of brilliant light with a voice "like the sound of a multitude" (Dan. 10:5–6).

Before she knew Jesus, Khalida had heard a voice inside telling her to "leave the darkness for the light" while her Muslim husband was beating her. But during her vision of Heaven, she heard Jesus speak with a "voice like *mighty rushing waters*, powerful and soothing at the same time," which she recognized as the same voice.[1]

Several other NDErs recall the voice of God:

When he spoke, it was like somebody had put it on a tremendous loudspeaker and it just bounced off the clouds: "Take her back." . . . The light was so beautiful! It was so bright all around the Lord, and his voice was so *commanding and yet gentle*.[2]

I heard a commanding voice that came from everywhere all at once. I even heard it inside of me. It sounded like a *thunderous clap of lightening* [sic], *a great wind and white water rapids* all rolled together, saying, "It's not your time!"[3]

The voice of God . . . was like the *voice of a hundred friends* talking in harmonious unison. . . . I was alarmed—until I listened to what he had to say. "Don't be afraid," God assured me. "You have nothing to fear. It's all going to be okay."[4]

All over the globe, those who experience God hear the same voice. Samaa, a Christian from the Middle East, heard this:

"Welcome home, Samaa," He said in a voice sweet and gentle, yet also powerful, *like the sound of many waters*. He opened His arms to me. His beautiful eyes were like blazing fires of consuming love that overwhelmed me.[5]

Imagine that day when you finally hear God's voice with loving power speaking straight to you. We long for God to speak to us in a way that is clear; however, most of the time he does not speak out loud. Rather, he speaks through his Word, in a quiet whisper, through a friend's loving encouragement, or in our thoughts.

It takes practice to know how to discern between God's voice and our own thoughts. Scheduling regular times to be in his Word and making space in your life for daily, proactive, conscious connection with God helps you decipher what his Spirit is saying and where he wants to guide you.

As you practice being mindful of his voice throughout the day, and as you obediently respond in faith, you will learn how to better discern when he is speaking to you. Today, every hour, check in with God, stop to listen, ask him to direct you, and obediently act in faith. You'll look back and see how he guides.[6]

Prayer: *Father, give me ears to hear your voice today. Help me learn to listen for your Spirit's prompting and obey in faith.*

58

You make known to me the path of life; you will fill me with
joy in your presence, with eternal pleasures at your right hand.

Psalm 16:11

FOURTEEN-YEAR-OLD HANNAH clinically died and arrived in
Heaven, still feeling timid and uncertain from being abused
in her past. She discovered a land of joyful laughter and was
invited in to experience pleasures she had never known.

At first, Hannah was mesmerized as she looked around and
saw "everything was alive with light and glowing. The trees and
every living plant and flower [were] pristine." Then she quickly
became tentative about where she might be allowed to go, since
she was in a new place, so she tried to hide behind a tree. To her
surprise and delight, when she thought about disappearing inside
the tree, she actually did!

Two women passed by, but she stayed hidden just in case she
was not supposed to be there. All of a sudden she heard a male
voice ask her, "Are you going to stay in the tree the whole time?"
This made her giggle, and she confessed that she didn't think she
could go anywhere else. The voice answered, "This is your home
and you can go anywhere you wish."

Hannah felt a newfound freedom and began to walk down a path
full of vibrant flowers and trees, doing gymnastics as she went along.
She was overjoyed when she realized she was tumbling perfectly, like
she had never been able to do before! It thrilled her heart to the core.

She stopped and turned around, and described seeing Jesus as
the one whose voice she had heard:

> There before me was the most BEAUTIFUL man I have ever seen in
> my whole life! The look on his face was pure LOVE and excitement.

I have never ever had anyone look at me like this. . . . His expression never chang[ed] from those wide eyes and contagious smile.

Hannah shares that, next, Jesus told her he wanted to show her something, so they got up, and he lead her hand in hand to another area of Heaven.

> There was a great multitude of people whose number I couldn't count. They were all smiling at me. . . . He said, "All these people love you." I said, "They do?!" Everyone was glowing with the colors of heaven. They were full of love and light and super excited to see me. They all told me telepathically they loved me and were proud of me. . . . I said to Jesus, "I wish I hadn't spent so much time in the tree, I could maybe have visited with them." I felt bad for not talking to those two women; knowing now how they all felt about me. Jesus started laughing about the tree comment. Everyone thought it was funny and laughed. It was so magical, and I will never forget it![1]

As the world seems to be in constant turmoil, stop and imagine the wonderful pleasures that await you in the life to come. Imagine the joy and delight that will envelop you, the loving fellowship that will surround you, and the new discoveries you can look forward to with hopeful anticipation.

No matter what you've been through or have had to endure in this life, hold on to the promises of God. He will fill you with the joy of his presence as you follow him. The eternal pleasures you will experience one day will far outweigh anything you are enduring on earth.

Today, focus on the sweet happiness of Heaven that awaits you, and the presence of God with you now. Let the Spirit of God fill you with his supernatural joy as you follow him.

Prayer: *God, thank you for your presence in my life today, and for pleasures to come. I want to delight in you always.*

59

To all who mourn in Israel, he will give a crown of beauty for ashes, a joyous blessing instead of mourning, festive praise instead of despair.

Isaiah 61:3 NLT

IMAGINE THE DAY God shows you how your faithful perseverance and loving acts of kindness produced an unseen ripple effect of good even out of life's tragedies.

Dr. Mary Neal felt Jesus's embrace as she relived her whole life while trapped underwater in her kayak.

My life was laid bare for all its good and bad. One of the things we did was look at many, many, many events throughout my life that I would have otherwise called terrible or horrible or sad or bad or tragic.

And, instead of looking at an event in isolation, or looking at how it impacted me and my little world, I had the most remarkable experience of seeing the ripple effects of the event when seen 25, 30, 35 times removed . . . [and how it] changed me and changed others such that again and again and again, I was shown that indeed, it is true: beauty comes of all things.

Jesus was showing me this and saying, "Look at how that event impacted this person that impacted that person that impacted that person." And, again and again, [Jesus] showed me that when you step outside yourself—when you step outside your perception of the world around you—that everything creates great beauty.

We can look at events or obstacles or setbacks in our own life that happened 10 years ago. You lose a job and you're devastated, but you look back 10 years and you're so grateful because loss of that job set you up for the next opportunity. And it was remarkable to be shown so many times the truth of that verse. The truth of God's promise that there really is beauty that comes from all things. . . . And it's trusting that that beauty is there regardless of whether I can see it or not.[1]

Through this experience, I was able to clearly see that every action, every decision, and every human interaction impacts the bigger world in far more significant ways than we could ever be capable of appreciating. It was really a life-changing experience.[2]

It is really remarkable to imagine the power one small act of kindness can have in God's economy, or how God can use an event we see as negative to actually produce a positive result we would never foresee. The ripple effect of good from your actions can bless generation after generation—you will never know the magnitude until you get to Heaven!

As believers in Jesus, it is so comforting to know that God will work everything that happens in our lives for ultimate good, no matter how bad things seem (Rom. 8:28). As you follow God through your journey, you can have peace with your circumstances, knowing that ultimately, through this ripple effect, a positive outcome will happen for someone, somehow, as God promises.

As Isaiah 61 says, God will make beauty from ashes, replace your mourning with blessing, and will harvest new praise from past despair. Even though this may not be in your earthly lifetime, holding on to this promise for generations that follow you can help you as you endure the hard times of the present.

Today, hold tightly to Jesus no matter what you are facing. You can be confident in the promise, knowing that good will prevail in the end.

Prayer: *Dear Father, thank you that you make beauty out of all things, good and bad, for all who love and follow you. Help me to hold on to your promise through the difficulties and trials of life.*

60

Judge nothing before the appointed time; wait until the Lord comes. He will bring to light what is hidden in darkness and will expose the motives of the heart. At that time each will receive their praise from God.

1 Corinthians 4:5

IMAGINE WHEN YOUR EARTHLY LIFE ENDS, and you re-experience your whole life from a new perspective. Researcher Steve Miller found that in Heaven, many NDErs were given insight and understanding into the "why" questions of life that so many of us struggle with here on earth:

My whole life so far appeared to be placed before me in a kind of panoramic, three-dimensional review, and each event seemed to be accompanied by an awareness of good and evil or by an insight into its cause and effect.

Throughout, I not only saw everything from my own point of view, but also I knew the thoughts of everybody who'd been involved in these events, as if their thoughts were lodged inside me. It meant that I saw not only what I had done or thought, but even how this had affected others, as if I was seeing with all-knowing eyes. And throughout, the review stressed the importance of love.

I can't say how long this life review and insight into life lasted; it may have been quite long because it covered every single subject, but at the same time it felt like a split second because I saw everything at once. It seemed as if time and distance didn't exist.

It was clear to me why I'd had cancer. Why I had come into this world in the first place. What role each of my family members played in my life, where we all were within the grand scheme of things, and in general what life is all about. The clarity and insight I had in that state are simply indescribable.[1]

Most of the NDErs Steve Miller studied said this perfect understanding was "veiled" once they returned to earth, perhaps because we are not meant to have full knowledge this side of Heaven.

There are so many times we ask the question "Why?" Life gets confusing, and it is not easy to make sense of the chaos that falls upon us, especially when we are choosing to honor God the best we know how.

Even so, you can rest in the fact that one day you will have complete understanding and resolution of all your questions. You will have all your doubt and confusion settled and replaced with the peace and contentment that everything is well with your soul.

It brings comfort to know that God is sovereign, and he will bring to light what is now in darkness. Your perseverance and faith during the "why" times will receive praise from him. He wants you to rest in the fact that he will ultimately make all things good and will reward your faithfulness to him.

Focus today on the truth that even though you may not understand everything now, you can trust God in the waiting. As Proverbs 3:5–6 says, "Trust in the LORD with all your heart; do not depend on your own understanding. Seek his will in all you do, and he will show you which path to take" (NLT).

Prayer: *Dear Heavenly Father, I have faith that one day you will reveal to me the answers to all my questions, and I can trust you in my questions and struggles. Thank you for guiding me as I seek your will for my life.*

61

Therefore I tell you, do not worry about your life. . . . Can any one of you by worrying add a single hour to your life? . . . But seek first his kingdom and his righteousness, and all these things will be given to you as well.

Matthew 6:25, 27, 33

PAT JOHNSON and his childhood friend, Bobby, went kayaking on the Blanco River. Pat's kayak hit a low-water bridge and turned sideways, and Pat recalls being pulled under:

I felt like a large giant had grabbed me by the ankles and pulled me under . . . I felt the ridges of a corrugated pipe bumping the backs of my hands. I immediately knew I was in a metal pipe. . . .While underwater, I only had three things on my mind and heart. I was praying, thinking about my kids and wife, and trying to survive. . . .

Everything got quiet, I didn't feel the water on my body, and I knew there was nothing to worry about. In that moment, I knew my family would be fine, and everything in the world was where it was supposed to be. Then, in an instant, like turning off a light switch, I lost consciousness and was in a different place. . . .

I knew I was where I was supposed to be. Nothing compares to it on earth. Immediately upon arriving at this other place, I was connected to a multitude of souls. I didn't see them, but I felt them, and I knew I was connected to them.

Pat saw a light in the distance, and as he got closer, he saw people walking around and felt a profound sense of belonging. At that moment, he regained consciousness after suddenly being pushed out of the pipe.

I went tumbling down the river pushed by the rapids. Bobby saw me bouncing down the river, and he jumped off the bridge to rescue me. . . . The experience affects Bobby to this day. And for the first two or three months after this happened, I felt like I could almost physically see people's souls.

It takes a long time to integrate this experience into your life, if you ever do. I don't think the lessons that you come back with ever leave you.

For me, the lessons and messages that I received were: the unconditional love of God, how connected we are to God and each other, the true value of all of us is "soul," and that God loves all of us the way we are, not for what we have or have done.

I think the most important message I received was that we are overthinking things. Just love God and love each other, and everything else will take care of itself.[1]

Because God is in control, there is nothing we need to worry about! So often we find ourselves stressed over a multitude of things, stewing over situations that don't ever happen the way we feared they would.

Even though we cannot add a day to our life by worrying, we often over-think and over-analyze to the point of creating problems in our minds that don't even exist. When you find yourself caught up in this, move your mind off the worries and onto God, releasing all your anxious thoughts to him. This will help calm your mind and bring peace to your situation. You can trust his love and care with even the smallest details of your life.

God wants you to be free of the worries that distract you from enjoying his blessings and experiencing your life abundantly, the way he desires. Today, turn your worries into prayers and give your concerns to God. Find comfort in knowing that he has everything under control!

Prayer: *Dear God, I turn my worries into prayers and give them to you to handle today. Help me to focus on loving you and loving others, trusting you will work your perfect will in my life.*

62

> He was pierced for our transgressions, he was crushed for our iniquities; the punishment that brought us peace was on him, and by his wounds we are healed.
>
> Isaiah 53:5

WHILE PLAYING WITH HIS DAD, four-year-old Colton made a curious comment: "Jesus has markers."

Todd asked if, by markers, he meant the kind Colton colored with.

Colton said, "Yeah, like colors. He had colors on him." When asked what color, he answered, "Red, Daddy. Jesus has red markers on him."

Todd felt overwhelmed with emotion as he suddenly understood what Colton was trying to say. He asked Colton where Jesus's markers were. Colton stood up, pointed to both hands, then at the tops of his feet. "That's where Jesus's markers are, Daddy."[1]

Richard, a Jewish man who believed in Jesus, died in an auto accident and claimed he observed light coming out of the nail holes. He said that Jesus "held out His hands in front of me, and I saw the nail scars. The wounds were open, shining with a beautiful light."[2]

As Gary stood before Jesus during his NDE, he noticed "where nails had been driven into His hands, not His palms as some paintings depict, but into His wrists." He also saw his friend healed by those same wounds:

> Suddenly, there in front of me stood my best friend. . . . His eyes sparkled with life as we embraced. . . . In heaven he is whole. If someone is blind here on earth, when they died, and if they go to heaven, they will be able to see. It is the same if someone is missing arms or legs, when they get to heaven they will be whole and complete.[3]

Don Piper realized the ultimate healing of Heaven when he saw his great-grandmother:

> My great-grandmother, Hattie Mann, was Native American. As a child I saw her only after she had developed osteoporosis. Her head and shoulders were bent forward, giving her a humped appearance. I especially remember her extremely wrinkled face. The other thing that stands out in my memory is that she had false teeth—which she didn't wear often. Yet when she smiled at me in heaven, her teeth sparkled. I knew they were her own, and when she smiled, it was the most beautiful smile I had ever seen. Then I noticed something else—she wasn't slumped over. She stood strong and upright, and the wrinkles had been erased from her face.[4]

Jesus carries his nail scars as a sign of victory that "by his wounds we are healed." His wounds have healed and still are healing all the effects of a broken, sin-stained world.

This is a promise we will fully experience forever in Heaven, but he is also healing us day by day as we learn to live in the victory of the cross and resurrection power of Jesus. Whatever challenges need healing in your life—your relationships, your body, your emotions, your broken heart—Jesus has the power to heal them.

Ultimately in Heaven, we will experience this promise of complete healing, but sometimes the healing of our souls is helped along through things unhealed now. Paul prayed for a physical malady to be healed: "Three different times I begged the Lord to take it away. Each time he said, 'My grace is all you need. My power works best in weakness'" (2 Cor. 12:8–9 NLT).

Today, pray in faith for healing for yourself or others who are suffering. You can also trust Jesus with the outcome, looking forward to the day in Heaven when all brokenness will be restored forever.

> **Prayer:** *Dear Jesus, by your wounds I am healed. Give me courage to trust your healing power over areas of brokenness in my life, believing you can make me stronger through my weakness.*

63

I urge you, first of all, to pray for all people. Ask God to help them; intercede on their behalf, and give thanks for them.

1 Timothy 2:1 NLT

AFTER THREE LONG WEEKS suffering in the hospital, Jack rolled over in bed to ease the pain. At that moment, a brilliant light appeared in the room and a serene peace came over him. A hand reached out of the light and a voice said, "Come with me. I want to show you something."

Jack reached out and took hold of the hand. Immediately, he experienced the feeling of being pulled away from his body and moving up toward the ceiling above. As he looked back, he could see his body still lying there on the bed. "We started moving through the ceiling and the wall of the hospital room . . . down to a lower floor in the hospital. We had no difficulty in passing through doors or walls," Jack recalled.

Jack discovered they had journeyed to the hospital recovery room, the location of which he had not known before. He also took note of the placement of the hospital beds in the room, and explained how this loving being told him which bed he was going to occupy in recovery. It was clear to Jack that God was showing him all this so he would not be afraid, especially since Jack had to go through several other things before his death. Jack shared he had a strong sense that God would be overseeing the whole process and would definitely be there with him at the end.

When Jack got up the next morning, knowing he would not survive the surgery, he was not at all afraid. Even though he knew he was going to die, "there was no regret, no fear. There was no thought, 'what can I do to keep this from happening?' I was ready."

The night before the surgery, Jack decided to write two letters and hide them—one for his wife and one for his nephew, whom he had legally adopted as his own son. About two pages into his letter to his wife, the floodgates opened, and he began to sob. As he cried uncontrollably, Jack again felt God's presence enter the room.

"Jack, why are you crying? I thought you would be pleased to be with me." Jack thought, "Yes, I am. I want to go very much." Jack told God that he was worried about his nephew and the difficulty his wife would face raising him alone. Jack tried to put his feelings into words, explaining that if he might have been around to assist his wife, he could have helped his nephew get through his setbacks and struggles. God's voice responded, "Since you're asking for someone else, and thinking of others, not Jack, I will grant you what you want. You will live until you see your nephew become a man."[1]

God is a relational, personal God. When you intercede in prayer for others, God delights in the compassion and love you are showing toward them. Scripture encourages us to pray for others—for their salvation, their healing, and their concerns. God listens to the cries of your heart on behalf of others. Sometimes he will change a course of action due to our heartfelt prayers (Isa. 38). It's mysterious how this works, but in his sovereignty, God chooses to allow us to take part in the workings of his will and ways. Because of this, you can pray with confidence that your requests do have effect on God's heart, and you can stand before the throne for others, even those who do not know him yet.

Every person is precious in the sight of God, and he gives you the privilege, through intercessory prayer, of helping those who don't know him. Today, take someone's cares to the throne. Pray that your requests will move the heart of God and affect positive change for your loved one.

> **Prayer:** Lord, thank you for being such a caring and compassionate Father. Help me to intercede for those who need your guidance and leadership, trusting that you will use my prayers to work your perfect will in their lives.

64

Make the most of every opportunity in these evil days. Don't act thoughtlessly, but understand what the Lord wants you to do.

Ephesians 5:16–17

STEVE SJOGREN was leading a large church doing lots of good, yet during his NDE God redirected him:

As the clock ticked, I heard God speak. He told me about my life and all that He wanted to change in it. It was as if we had taken a trip to the woodshed, in the most positive sense of the expression. God gave me a number of life-altering, unforgettable messages that I will take to my grave. . . .

We did not communicate just with words, but also with memories and images. God let me know how much He valued me. It's almost impossible to describe the perfect sense of acceptance that surrounded me, yet even in the midst of this very personal embrace, part of me knew that not everything in my life had matched what God had intended for me. I had fallen down so often that the angels probably had headaches.

Despite my list of fiascos, God extended His total acceptance and absolute love to me—and showed me how He was going to give me another chance. I got the sense that God was going to give me an opportunity to let go of the things that had become idols in my life and allow me to begin to embrace people instead. I was to become the husband and father that I was supposed to be. I was to become the employer, neighbor and friend that I was intended to be.[1]

Lindi, a mother of three, shared this about her experience:

I was always afraid of judgment. I know there's no condemnation for those in Christ, but because of all my past sin, I knew I'd be held to account. So honestly, I wasn't really excited about Heaven.

But when I was there, it wasn't like that—I was so excited for my life review.

I heard a Voice [assumed from Jesus] giving another person a life review, saying, "Let's look at all the things you've done to serve Me, to love other people well; let's look at the relationships in your life and how you've loved them well and therefore served Me through them." What was interesting is it was all about relationships. There was nothing about accomplishments, nothing about our "successes"—all about how you've loved other people.

Then the Voice said, "Let's look at how you could have loved other people better, and the missed relationships, and how you could have loved them better and therefore served Me better." Then the Voice said, "Welcome home, thank you for loving me so well throughout your life."[2]

Lindi realized there's truly no condemnation, and it motivated her to not miss opportunities.

The world tells us money matters, power matters, and prestige matters—and we often run ourselves ragged trying to prove to one another and to ourselves that we're successful enough, important enough, or powerful enough. In contrast, our relationships are what truly matter most to God, and he loves and accepts us just as we are.

As you go about your life, be mindful of opportunities God gives you to live for what truly matters. Be generous with your resources, steward your positions and prestige wisely for his glory, and invest in people's lives.

Today, seek out ways to bless others and love them with God's love. All it takes is being willing before God, and he will show you those who need his love and encouragement.

> **Prayer:** *Jesus, help me steward my time and resources well and to see the relationships in my life as a priority, knowing that these are what last and are most important to you.*

65

There is no fear in love. But perfect love drives out fear, because fear has to do with punishment. The one who fears is not made perfect in love.

1 John 4:18

As AN ATHEIST, HOWARD STORM lived most of his life set against God. Yet in his moments of dying, he cried out to Jesus to save him. Now as he watched his life review, he was deeply ashamed of the choices he had made apart from God. Even so, Jesus and the angels consistently communicated only unconditional love for him.

> No matter what we watched me do in life, they communicated their deep love for me, even as they expressed their disapproval of things I did. One of the things I had done repeatedly in my life was blaspheme God. . . . I was horrified at how it hurt my heavenly company when we witnessed me blaspheming God and Christ Jesus in my life review.[1]

Even though Howard knew he had grieved the heart of God, he felt Jesus reassuring him that he was still loved.

> He made perfectly clear what he did not like—and I can safely say, despised, hated, detested, what I had done with my life—but he always loved me. And the reason why he didn't love what I did was because it distracted from who I was meant to be.
>
> That's why he didn't like it. When you see someone that not only is not living up to their potential but actually denying their potential—because I was made for one purpose and one purpose only and that's what I was missing. I was made to love God with all my heart, mind, soul, and strength, to love my neighbor as myself. Three things: love God, love my neighbor, love myself. And that they are so intertwined that you can't do one without the other.

The angels showed me that we do not earn our love of God by the things we do. God's love is given without cost or strings attached. We live lovingly because God loves us so much. Thank God there is a way to change our lives and be forgiven our mistakes. The next time I leave this world, I will be able to stand with the angels and Jesus Christ and look at my life without constant shame and foreboding.[2]

Most NDErs experience a life review in God's presence, as he gently guides them to see what matters most in life. Usually, they are asked a question by the Lord first: "What have you done with the life I gave you?" It is said in love, to prompt reflection and learning.

Your Heavenly Father wants to reward you for the ways you have honored him and loved others through him. God does not want you to live in fear of punishment. He wants you to live out of the confidence of his unconditional love in Christ, living your life to delight his heart.

It's not difficult to please him; all you need to do is walk by faith in a desire to love God, being willing to follow his lead. As a believer, you have already been forgiven for your past, present, and future, and that will never change. For this reason, let his overwhelming love and mercy be your motivation to want to please him.

Today, find opportunities to live for what truly matters, confident in God's relentless love for you. How thrilling to look forward to a review of your life one day, celebrating with Jesus the positive effects of your loving actions in countless lives!

> **Prayer:** *Heavenly Father, as I reflect on what I've done with the life you gave me, help me to prioritize what is most on your heart and to please you in all I do. Thank you for your love.*

66

> Nothing impure will ever enter [the Holy City], nor will anyone who does what is shameful or deceitful, but only those whose names are written in the Lamb's book of life.
>
> Revelation 21:27

I T IS INTERESTING how many NDErs refer to the books of Heaven. After marveling at the beauty of Paradise, Gary made his way up to the city gate.

> [An] angel came through the gate, and he was checking the pages of a book that he was carrying. He then nodded to the giant angel, confirming that I may enter into the city. . . . I later learned that we are all assigned a loved one, who is already in heaven, to acquaint us to this place called heaven, and [my deceased best friend] John was the one assigned to me. . . . .
>
> John told me he had many wonderful things to show me. John took me into a very large building that looked like a library. The walls were solid gold and sparkled with a dazzling display of light that loomed up high to a crystal, domed ceiling. I saw hundreds and hundreds of volumes of books. . . . Many angels were there reading the contents of the books. John explained to me that these books contain a record of every person's life that has ever been born, throughout all history. Everything we do here on earth is recorded in these books—good or bad—everything.[1]

Thirteen-year-old Barbara, who died in a pool accident, found herself at the city gates where she saw books and an "old" friend:

> I was waiting in line at first, behind all these people. And then it was my turn. And I was standing in front of this BIG guy, who I think was an angel. He was holding this BIG book. . . . The angel guy asked me for my name, and I told him. When he looked for it he said, "I'm sorry but it is not your time." So I said to him,

"Why is it not my time?!?! I'm ready to die! My life sucks!! My best friend died [five] years ago!! Why is it not my time?!?!" Then he pointed to the gate with the city behind it. . . . It was Jake, my best friend, [who] died in a car accident five years ago. We were both seven years old, and when I saw him there I ran to the gate as fast as I could. . . . Then we talked for a while, about things that happened, about each other, and then the angel said, "It's time for you to go back."[2]

Another teenager who drowned explains that he also saw books:

Moment by moment you discover how quickly you are gaining knowledge; and how easy it is to accept. My three angels sought permission from above to show me something. . . . What looked like a HUGE four-foot-thick book, of LIFE. MY Life. Just as my life had passed before my eyes when I was being drowned, I was now being shown my future life.[3]

There are books in Heaven recording our deeds, and a separate Book of Life that holds the names of those who belong to God and where the days of our lives are recorded. The psalmist says, "Your eyes saw my unformed body; all the days ordained for me were written in your book before one of them came to be" (Ps. 139:16).

You can have confidence and assurance that God's plan for you is perfect and his timing is right, and your time has not finished yet on earth. God has a divine purpose for your life, one that only you can fulfill in the ways he intended.

Approach each day with the knowledge that you are here for a reason, to carry out the will of your Creator and to live out the abundant life Jesus came to give. Today, live with purpose, confident that you have a significant role to play in God's grand plan for the world.

> **Prayer:** *Lord, thank you for giving my life purpose and meaning. Help me to make a difference for you during my time here on earth.*

67

For Christ's love compels us. . . . [H]e died for all, that those who live should no longer live for themselves. . . . God was reconciling the world to himself in Christ, not counting people's sins against them. And he has committed to us the message of reconciliation.

2 Corinthians 5:14–15, 19

AFTER THE COLD STEEL of a terrorist's bomb ripped through Samaa during a church service in a Middle Eastern country, she recalls this:

Thrown ten feet into the air and smashed against the opposite wall, I called out to Jesus silently in my agony: "Jesus, help me!" And then, in that instant, my spirit left my body and I died. . . .

When I opened my eyes, I saw brilliant white light illuminating Jesus, the Son of Man, the Son of God. His face was brighter than the sun, and He was so glorious. . . . It was as if Jesus could see through me, reading all the thoughts of my heart. My whole body was shaking. I felt so unworthy to be in His presence. . . . He radiated an amazing love that contained deep acceptance. I felt neither condemnation nor shame. . . .

"Welcome home, Samaa," He said in a voice sweet and gentle, yet also powerful, like the sound of many waters. He opened His arms to me. His beautiful eyes were like blazing fires of consuming love that overwhelmed me. Like a magnet, His love drew me in. . . .

"Do you want to go back or stay here in heaven?" Jesus asked. Then He showed me my life. As if seeing snapshots of a movie, I watched myself growing up. The nineteen years I'd lived passed in front of my eyes. After seeing the choices I had made, I realized I had been living for my own agenda and repented.

Oh, Lord Jesus, I'm so sorry. Please forgive me. All my life I've been living for myself—my ways, my dreams, my desires, my plans. But it's not about me. It's all about You. . . . He wanted me to go back for my family, for their salvation, but also for the salvation of His family, which is multitudes! God is all about family, from Genesis to Revelation. As Revelation 5:9 says: "You are worthy to take the scroll and to open its seals, because you were slain, and with your blood you purchased for God persons from every tribe and language and people and nation." . . . He is also a Gentleman. He never forced me but gave me the freedom to choose. As I told Him my choice—that I wanted to go back to earth and be a witness for Him—I was motivated by love, not a sense of duty. . . .

"All right, see you soon," He said.

Immediately a fresh wave of love washed over me. It felt so easy to talk to Him, to communicate, like a child speaking to her Father.[1]

Through the cross, Jesus paid the ultimate human price to forgive and restore relationship with every willing person. Jesus loves us so much that he suffered on our behalf so that all people could come home to God. There are so many people in the world longing for the hope and peace that only come through Jesus, and they are just waiting to grab hold of the peace and joy he offers.

God has given every believer the ministry of reconciliation, the assignment to help others experience his love and forgiveness in their lives. What a privilege we have to partner with him to help guide others into a restored relationship with their Heavenly Father!

As you think about this, ask God to bring to mind those in your life who don't know him, and pray for a time to share God's love and forgiveness with them. Let his overwhelming love

Prayer: *Dear God, thank you for the gift of salvation. I want to love you by being a messenger of reconciliation, openly sharing your love and forgiveness with those you put in my path who do not know you.*

68

God was reconciling the world to himself in Christ, not counting people's sins against them. And he has committed to us the message of reconciliation. We are therefore Christ's ambassadors, as though God were making his appeal through us. We implore you on Christ's behalf: Be reconciled to God.

2 Corinthians 5:19–20

HELPING PEOPLE FIND FAITH and grow spiritually will one day bring you great, great joy! You don't have to be far along to simply reach back and help someone two steps behind you. Ian McCormack got this message after calling out for Jesus to save him during his dying breaths:

Directly behind Jesus was a circular shaped opening like the tunnel I had just traveled down. Gazing out through it, I could see a whole new world opening up before me. I felt like I was standing on the edge of paradise. . . .

Through the centre of the meadows I could see a crystal clear stream winding its way across the landscape with trees on either bank. To my right were mountains in the distance and the sky above was blue and clear. . . .

Jesus asked me this question: "Ian, now that you have seen, do you wish to return?" I thought, "Return, of course not. Why would I want to go back? Why would I want to return to the misery and hatred? No, I have nothing to return for. I have no wife or kids, no one who really loves me. You are the first person who has ever truly loved me. . . ."

But he didn't move so I looked back one last time to say, "Goodbye cruel world, I'm out of here!" As I did, in a clear vision right in front of the tunnel, stood my mother. As I saw her I realised my mistake; there was one person who loved me—my dear Mum. . . . I had mocked her beliefs. But she had been right after all, there was a God and a heaven and a hell.

I began to consider how selfish it would be to go through to paradise and leave my mother believing that I had gone to hell. . . . So I said, "God, there's only one person really I want to go back for and that is my mum." . . .

Then as I looked back again, I saw behind her my father, my brother and sister, my friends, and a multitude of other people. God was showing me that there were many other people who also didn't know, and would never know unless I was able to share with them. I responded, "I don't love those people" but he replied, "I love them and I desire all of them to come to know me." Then the Lord said, "If you return you must see things in a new light."[1]

Sharing the good news of Jesus Christ is something that all Christ followers must be prepared to do. In fact, the gospel is the best news we can offer anyone! It not only secures their eternity; it enables them to experience the unconditional love and guidance of God while facing the challenges of life today.

Too often, it is easier to shy away from sharing our faith. Yet telling others about Jesus is more important than talking about anything else. As an ambassador for Christ, you represent him to those he leads into your life. You bring his love and acceptance to them through your words and actions, pointing them to the Savior.

Take some time today to reflect on who God may be putting on your heart to serve, share Christ with, or develop. One day you will see how your greatest impact on humanity came by leading your family and friends to Christ and developing them to become all God intended.

Prayer: *Heavenly Father, please help me to be a true ambassador for you, leading others into the joy of your salvation and helping them become the people you intend them to be.*

69

And if I go and prepare a place for you, I will come back
and take you to be with me that you also may be where I am.

John 14:3

REFLECTING ON HER EXPERIENCE OF HEAVEN, Crystal—
who had been baptized but never felt loved due to the abuse
she suffered—admits it is challenging to find the right words
to describe what she saw, simply because human language doesn't
even come close. Words like *beautiful, brilliant,* and *amazing* fall
far short, she says.

> What I experienced in heaven was so real and so lucid and so ut-
> terly intense, it made my experiences on Earth seem hazy and out
> of focus—as if heaven is the reality and life as we know it is just
> a dream"

Crystal describes being immersed in a feeling of complete and
utter purity, perfection, unbrokenness, and peace—a kind of assurance she's never experienced on earth.

> It was like being bathed in love," [she remembers]. "It was a bright-
> ness I didn't just see, but felt. And it felt familiar, like something
> I remembered, or even recognized. The best way to put it is this:
> I was home.[1]

Jeff Olsen also experienced this sense of home during his fatal
car accident:

> [I] was in a different place. This was a place of joy. It was familiar.
> It was home. I felt real, but I was not injured. I was not a floating
> orb. I was myself.[2]

Don Piper, who spent ninety minutes clinically dead, says:

> I saw colors I would never have believed existed. I've never, ever felt more alive than I did then. I was home; I was where I belonged. I wanted to be there more than I had ever wanted to be anywhere on earth."[3]

In Heaven, you will feel more alive, more real, more at home than you ever have on earth. Jesus claimed that God's heart is that of a loving Father who would do anything to have his kids come home.

One day he will welcome you home too! And home is the place where you will finally be fully known and perfectly loved, surrounded by family and friends who delight in being with you. You will feel like you were made for this home and it was made for you. You will feel a belonging like never before.

Whenever you feel alone, out of place, alienated, or like you don't belong—find hope and comfort in God's promises that you do belong. One day you will be in your true home forever. Let this motivate you now to live for God fully, helping others know they belong, and invite them into his loving family to join you there.

Prayer: *Heavenly Father, help me to realize that this world is not my final home, and that you have prepared a wonderful place for me in heaven. Help me to invite others into that home to join me for eternity.*

70

About that time the disciples came to Jesus and asked, "Who is greatest in the Kingdom of Heaven?" Jesus called a little child to him and put the child among them. Then he said, "I tell you the truth, unless you turn from your sins and become like little children, you will never get into the Kingdom of Heaven. So anyone who becomes as humble as this little child is the greatest in the Kingdom of Heaven. And anyone who welcomes a little child like this on my behalf is welcoming me."

Matthew 18:1–5 NLT

SAM IS A GOOD FRIEND whose grown child, Shane, has both autism and severe mental disabilities. He doesn't understand abstract things like Heaven. One Saturday morning, Shane came downstairs and announced, "I'm getting baptized at church Sunday." That piqued Sam's interest, because she was concerned Shane could not understand the significance of baptism.

"Maybe someday, but I don't think you have to get baptized," Sam said.

"No, I do! Jesus told me I'm going to get baptized on Sunday," Shane insisted.

Sam was concerned. "Shane, Jesus didn't tell you that!"

Shane, who had never ever mentioned a dream in his life, proclaimed, "No, I had a dream last night and Jesus took me to Heaven, and Mamaw was there [Shane's deceased grandmother] and Jesus was there and God was there."

Sam knew something strange had happened; Shane couldn't make up abstract ideas like dreams or Heaven. Cautiously, Sam probed. "Well, what was it like?"

Shane excitedly explained, "Jesus built me a house, and it has a red door. He showed me my house and told me I'm getting baptized tomorrow."

Sam didn't even know if there was a baptism the next day. Still not sure what to think, she questioned, "He showed you your house? So Shane, will I live next to you?" Sam knew Shane loved to do everything with her.

"No!" came Shane's surprising answer.

"Well, why not?" Sam asked, quite shocked at his response.

"I'm living right next to God."

Shane got baptized the next day at our church's baptism, just like he said he would.[1]

It would make perfect sense if the Shanes of the world have the most special location in the City of God. Jesus said, "Blessed are the pure in heart, for they will see God" (Matt. 5:8).

Every believer will see God and experience the loving wonders of his presence. All it takes is the simple, childlike, trusting obedience we're all capable of displaying. This genuine and pure faith is the currency of Heaven, yet so often we make it more complicated than it really is.

Childlike trust makes us great in the kingdom of God. When you depend on God as a child depends on a loving parent, with an innocence and purity that displays unreserved trust, he will work powerfully in your life and reward you forever.

Today, in whatever trial you are enduring, rely on God with pure and simple trust like a child, for he is faithful. When you humbly go before him, you will feel strengthened through his powerful presence in your life.

Prayer: *Father in Heaven, thank you for your presence. I want to trust you with pure and simple faith like a child, to see more of your power and strength in my life.*

71

[These little ones] have angels who are always looking into the face of My Father in heaven.

Matthew 18:10 NLV

GOD APPOINTS ANGELS to protect and watch over his children on earth. Alexa was giving birth to her son when she began losing too much blood, and the birth took a different turn:

> I was suddenly above my body! It seemed the most natural thing in the world! I had hands, feet, and everything was as normal; I was me in some sort of soft gown. Even as I had lifted out of my body, there were Beings on both sides of me . . . these were the BIG guys—HUGE, POWERFUL Angels, with even more powerful white feathered wings. . . .
>
> I wanted to touch those wings so much; they looked so soft. . . . As I reached, the Angels started to escort me; that was their job . . . and to keep me safe (from what? I wondered). . . . The Angels glowed softly, and I had no fear.[1]

Bank president Marv Besteman experienced a calming presence from his angels:

> Don't ask me how I knew the two strangers who had just walked into my hospital room were angels; I just knew they were. Beyond any doubt, these were angelic visitors, come to take me home. I wasn't one bit worried about it, either. A feeling of deep calm washed over me as these two men approached my bed, one on either side of me. They were smiling and quiet. My angels looked like regular guys, except regular guys usually don't wear white robes.[2]

Crystal felt deep love and friendship from her angels:

> There was so much brightness coming off them that I couldn't make out any features. . . . [T]hey definitely had a form, which was roughly that of a human body: long and slender. The being on the right appeared a bit bigger than the one on the left. They didn't move or hover or anything—they were just there.
>
> And what I instantly felt for them was love. A great, sweeping love for my angels overwhelmed me. It was like they were the best friends I could ever have, though the word friend doesn't come close to describing them. I felt like they had been a part of my existence and my journey forever.[3]

Even though we cannot always see our angels in the spiritual realm, they are with us and often protect us in profound ways. Being aware of their presence, and knowing they are sent from God to help us, can give us courage and support during times when we need assistance or protection.

We are not to seek guidance from angels, only from God who instructs them. Psalm 91:11 teaches, "He will command his angels concerning you to guard you"; therefore, we can trust that God is in charge.

When you feel alone, know that God has his angels near you to guard you and help you. Even though you cannot always see them or recognize them, they are there. They carry out God's plan, and they are sent to minister to you in your time of need.

Today, no matter what you are going through, find comfort in knowing that you have angels nearby watching out for you. They are protecting and guarding you, sent by your Heavenly Father who loves you and cares for your every concern.

> **Prayer:** *Thank you, Father, for sending your angels to protect me in my times of need here on earth, and help me to find comfort in their ministering presence.*

72

You will seek me and find me when you seek me with all your heart.

Jeremiah 29:13

IN 1971, THREE-YEAR-OLD KATIE had a near-death experience during which she claims, "I clearly left my body and existed outside it." That experience still motivates her years later. She explains:

> I was in the kitchen eating nuts, when one cashew went down my windpipe. I turned blue and passed out. My family saw this and tried to revive me, but was unable to do so. I was dead for five minutes.
>
> My Mother called 911, but it was winter and the ambulance was unable to come for thirty minutes. My grandfather was a firefighter, so he knew what to do, but nothing worked on me. . . . My grandfather said that there was nothing else he could do. He pronounced me "dead."
>
> When I died, I rose above my body and saw my grandfather working on my body. My body was of no interest to me; instead, I moved out of the room towards a presence I felt in the living room area.
>
> I went towards this presence, which was within a brilliant, sunlight bright, light space—not a tunnel, but an area. The presence was unbelievable peace, love, acceptance, calm, and joy. The presence enveloped me and my joy was indescribable—as I write this, I am brought back to this emotion and it delights me still. The feeling is spectacular.
>
> I did not experience this presence as God (I was too young to understand the concept) but I did experience this presence as that which made me. I knew, without a doubt that I was a made creature, a being that owed its existence to this presence.

I do not remember reentering my body.

When I woke up the next day, I knew two things for sure: Firstly, that there is life after death. Secondly, that I was a created being. I did not know this as a rational knowledge, but rather I expressed this by pestering my mother with question after question: Who made me? What was eternity? And what was God? She was unable to answer my questions, but was wise enough to let me talk to others who could.

This experience moved me so deeply that I have dedicated my life to looking for answers to my questions through the study [of] both philosophy and religion. I am currently working on a doctorate in theology.[1]

Some seek God after a near-death experience, but some don't. Unfortunately, just because people have an experience of Heaven doesn't mean they will process their encounters in ways that will lead them closer to God.

For instance, some seek knowledge to re-create the experience rather than seek God personally, and as a result, they may venture into practices the Bible warns against: "Do not turn to mediums or seek out spiritists, or you will be defiled by them. I am the LORD your God" (Lev. 19:31).

God gives us freedom, and he loves to help those who are purposefully following after him. As 2 Chronicles 16:9 (NLT) says, "The eyes of the LORD search the whole earth in order to strengthen those whose hearts are fully committed to him." Fully commit your heart to him today, seeking to know God better, follow God closer, and love God more by responding when he prompts you to love, serve, or encourage others.

Watch how he will begin to fill your heart with his spiritual discernment and strength as you choose to seek him only.

Prayer: *Lord, thank you for first seeking me! Help me to truly seek you, the one true God, and trust in you with all my heart throughout the day.*

73

Take delight in the LORD, and he will give you the desires of your heart. Commit your way to the LORD; trust in him and he will do this: he will make your righteous reward shine like the dawn, your vindication like the noonday sun.

Psalm 37:4–6

THOSE WHO HAVE DIFFICULTY picturing Heaven often fear it will be boring. Just imagine the exhilarating future that awaits you as God's reward for a life well lived! As Captain Dale Black describes, we have never experienced a gift so great:

> To experience something so sacred, so profound as the boundless love of God was the most thrilling part of heaven. It satisfied a longing in the deepest part of me. My spiritual family had shared God's perfect love with me. How could I ever be the same? . . .
>
> I felt so special, you can't believe how special. After all, all this was for me. Everyone there was there for me. I had no idea what gift I was to receive, but the anticipation on the faces of the people let me know that it was something extraordinary. I felt like a kid again, like that fifth-grade kid who loved God. Like that kid who used to look forward to Christmas like you wouldn't believe. I couldn't wait to open the gifts that waited for me under the tree. And I couldn't wait for the gift that waited for me now.
>
> The music continued, such beautiful music, and I became even more excited. It swelled and with it so did my anticipation. And then, as I was about to travel through the entrance and receive the gift . . . I was swept away.[1]

Don Piper also spoke of the greatest longings of our hearts being finally fulfilled in Heaven:

> Everything I saw was bright—the brightest colors my eyes had ever beheld—so powerful that no earthly human could take in this

brilliance. In the midst of that powerful scene, I continued to step closer to the gate and assumed that I would go inside. My friends and relatives were all in front of me, calling, urging, and inviting me to follow. . . .

Just as I reached the gate, my senses were even more heightened, and I felt deliriously happy. I paused—I'm not sure why—just outside the gate. I was thrilled at the prospect and wanted to go inside. I knew everything would be even more thrilling than what I had experienced so far. At that very moment I was about to realize the yearning of every human heart.

I was in heaven and ready to go in through the pearlescent gate.[2]

When we get to Heaven, we will gain the greatest gift ever—eternal life with Jesus and with other believers who have gone before us. Your Father in Heaven will one day fulfill the deepest longings and desires of your heart. Confident of this, you can trust him with your circumstances, knowing that your reward is coming.

There will be no hardships in the life to come. All the struggles will be gone—no more misunderstandings, discontentment, hurt, resentment, loneliness, or pain. Instead, you will be surrounded by beauty and filled to overflowing with unconditional love, joy, peace, and perfect unity with your family and friends in heaven.

As you picture what awaits you, take delight in God today. Trust him with whatever lies ahead. Commit your way to him, follow his lead, and you can be confident that it will be more than worth it in the end.

> **Prayer:** *Father, in this life there are so many unmet desires of my heart, but I want to trust you with all of them. I commit my way to you today, and I'll follow you, knowing one day you will fulfill my deepest desires.*

74

Well done, good and faithful servant! You have been faithful
with a few things; I will put you in charge of many things.
Come and share your master's happiness!

Matthew 25:21

JESUS SHOWED GEORGE RITCHIE what appeared to be the outer
environs of Heaven, filled with people enraptured in their projects. "Enormous buildings stood in a beautiful sunny park, and
there was a relationship between the various structures, a pattern
to the way they were arranged, that reminded me somewhat of a
well-planned university."

Jesus led him into one of the buildings with high-ceilinged
corridors—it was buzzing with excitement, as if everyone was on
the verge of some great new breakthrough.

Somehow I felt that some vast experiment was being pursued, perhaps dozens and dozens of such experiments.

"What are they doing, Jesus?" I asked.

But although Knowing flamed from Him like fire—though, in
fact, I sensed that every activity on this mighty "campus" had
its source in God—no explanation lighted my mind. What was
communicated, as before, was love: compassion for my ignorance,
understanding that encompassed all my non-understanding.

And something more. . . . In spite of His obvious delight in the
beings around us, I sensed that even this was not the ultimate, that
He had far greater things to show me if only I could see. . . . We
entered a studio where music of a complexity I could not begin to
follow was being composed. . . .

Next we walked through a library the size of the whole University of Richmond. . . . *Here*, the thought occurred to me, *are
assembled the important books of the universe*. Immediately I
knew this was impossible. How could books be written somewhere

beyond the earth! But the thought persisted, although my mind rejected it. *The key works of the universe.*

They walked out of that building, across a park, and into a building that was crowded with technological machinery. It appeared to be a space observatory.

"Is this heaven, Lord Jesus?" I ventured. The calm, the brightness, they were surely heaven-like! So was the absence of self, of clamoring ego. "When these people were on earth, did they grow beyond selfish desires?"

They grew, and they have kept on growing. The answer shone like sunlight in that intent and eager atmosphere. But if growth could continue, then this was not all. Then there must be something even these serene beings lacked.[1]

Imagine if we keep on discovering, learning, and creating in Heaven because God's infinite wonders will take ages of eternity to explore! Maybe in Heaven we will understand earth's current mysteries in full, but we will forever learn and explore the mysteries of God.

It is exciting to think that all the hobbies, skills, and interests we enjoy here on earth will be developed in even greater depth in Heaven. Perhaps for you that may be art, technology, writing, cooking, fitness, research, music, teaching, serving, or any other gift God has given you.

One thing is definite: you will never finish exploring all the depths of God's creative capacities! And part of the reward of Heaven may encompass the various projects, responsibilities, creative endeavors, or exciting assignments God will give his faithful servants.

As you do your work today, imagine what you might do in Heaven that will continue to inspire you to even greater creative capacities while you work faithfully to please God.

Prayer: *Father, thank you that developing in my areas of interest and work pleases you, and it all counts for eternal enjoyment in Heaven!*

75

One thing I ask from the LORD, this only do I seek: that I may
dwell in the house of the LORD all the days of my life, to gaze
on the beauty of the LORD and to seek him in his temple.

Psalm 27:4

For you have rescued me from death; you have kept my feet
from slipping. So now I can walk in your presence, O God,
in your life-giving light.

Psalm 56:13 NLT

WE MAY NOT UNDERSTAND IT NOW like the prophet
David who wrote these psalms, but there's no greater
reward in all of creation than intimacy with God. He
is the light, love, and life of the universe and the innermost desire
of every heart. No one ever wants to leave his presence.

Dean Braxton describes being with this magnificent light and
love of Christ:

It was pure joy. Jesus is pure light! His brightness was before me,
around me, part of me, and in me. He is brighter than the noonday
sun, but we can still look at Him in Heaven. . . . Jesus is more beautiful, wonderful, and glorious than I can explain. I stopped looking
at Him with my eyes and saw Him as He is—from my heart. . . .

I was in Jesus, and Jesus was shining out of me. I would see
the brightness. The brightness was around me. I was part of the
brightness, and brightness was shining out of me. All of it was life.
I just wanted to praise Him forever. . . .

Everything about Jesus is love. His love for you is so personal
it seems as if it is only for you. You come to realize that He has
cared for you forever and will continue to care for you forever.
Jesus loves us completely. I knew He loved others, but it seemed as
if I was the only one.[1]

Imagine the most majestic, beautiful, awe-inspiring Being, who possesses such power that one word alone speaks into existence whole universes. Imagine this brilliant, beautiful light of God to whom all beauty, joy, and pleasure owe their existence.

And now imagine feeling a unique, close intimacy with that person—a closeness that rivals all other relational intimacies, unites all people, and takes away all the mourning, crying, and pain of our past. In the presence of Jesus, you will experience the deepest, most genuine, lavish, unconditional love you could ever imagine—and it will be given to you as if you were the only person ever created.

Jesus offers his presence to you now, here on earth. He desires to fill you to overflowing through the Holy Spirit, who dwells within every believer. Draw near to him in worship, and soak in his amazing love right now. Let yourself feel his love and light guiding your life today.

> **Prayer**: *Dear Jesus, thank you for your love for me. I long to experience a greater intimacy with you. Thank you for the gift of your Holy Spirit dwelling within me, and help me walk in the light of your presence every day.*

76

I pray that you, being rooted and established in love, may
have power, together with all the Lord's holy people, to grasp
how wide and long and high and deep is the love of Christ,
and to know this love that surpasses knowledge.

Ephesians 3:17–19

DURING HIS NEAR-DEATH EXPERIENCE while scuba diving,
Ian McCormack emerged from the end of a "tunnel" and
was standing before "the source of all the light and power."

My whole vision was taken up with this incredible light. It looked
like a white fire or a mountain of cut diamonds sparkling with the
most indescribable brilliance. . . .

A voice spoke to me from the centre of the light. It was the same
voice that I had heard earlier in the evening [guiding him in the
Lord's Prayer]. The voice said, "Ian, do you wish to return? . . ." I
replied, "If I am out of my body I don't know where I am, I wish
to return." The response from this person was, "If you wish to
return, Ian, you must see in a new light."

The moment I heard the words "see in a new light," something
clicked. I remembered being given a Christmas card, which said,
"Jesus is the light of the world," and "God is light and there is no
darkness in him." . . . So this was God! He is light. He knew my
name and he knew the secret thoughts of my heart and mind. I
thought, if this is God then he must also be able to see everything
I've ever done in my life.

I felt totally exposed and transparent before God. You can wear
masks before other people but you can't wear a mask before God.
. . . To my amazement a wave of pure unconditional love flowed
over me. It was the last thing I expected. Instead of judgment I
was being washed with pure love. Pure, unadulterated, clean, un-
inhibited, undeserved, love. It began to fill me up from the inside
out. . . . This love was healing my heart and I began to understand

that there is incredible hope for humankind in this love. I was so close I wondered if I could just step into the light that surrounded God and see him face to face. . . .

Standing in the centre of the light stood a man with dazzling white robes reaching down to his ankles. . . . I could see his bare feet. His garments were not manmade fabrics but were like garments of light. . . . I looked towards his face. It was so bright; it seemed to be about ten times brighter than the light I'd already seen. It made the sun look yellow and pale in comparison. It was so bright that I couldn't make out the features of his face. . . .

I knew that I was standing in the presence of Almighty God—no one but God could look like this.[1]

Every form of love we experience on earth, no matter how wonderful, is merely a drop in the ocean of love God created for you to experience with him. Even though humanity turns away from God, his love pursues us relentlessly.

No matter how hard we try, we can never fully grasp how high, long, or wide his great love is for us! As you receive and meditate on how loved you are, God's desire is that it sinks down deep into your roots so that you are like a strong, healthy, fruit-bearing tree (Eph. 3:17). Nothing can shake you because you are rooted in his amazing love that can never be taken away.

Today, focus your mind on God's relentless love for you. Let his love flow deep into your soul, saturating you with peace and joy that covers over your every care.

> **Prayer:** *Father, help me to understand the magnitude of your great love for me. I want my roots to be strong and secure in your love so I can live to the fullest, reflecting the same love to others.*

77

I am the way and the truth and the life. No one comes to the
Father except through me. If you really know me, you will
know my Father as well. From now on, you do know him
and have seen him.

John 14:6–7

K HALIDA WANDERED THE STREETS of Bethlehem as a child,
orphaned by a missile that took the lives of her whole
family. Sold into slavery, she traveled the Arab world with
a Bedouin tribe and was forced to marry a very abusive Muslim
man. Her husband eventually beat her and left her for dead, taking
her only daughter with him.

Later, she married a man who took her to the United States.
When her life was threatened by her second husband's beatings,
she managed to flee with her two children, homeless and penniless.

A Christian woman saw Khalida's plight and offered her a job
and a home, telling Khalida of the love of God found through
Jesus. Khalida wanted the love this woman had and asked Jesus
to show her if he was God. She claims she had a vision of Heaven:

A person was standing in front of me, but different from any person
I'd ever known. I heard His voice—it was the same voice I heard years
before. Though I didn't know who it was then [while still in Palestine],
He said over and over to me when my Muslim husband was beating me and threatening my life, "Leave the darkness for the light."

[Now] He said in Arabic, "I am the truth, the life, and the way,
and no one comes to the Father except by Me." His voice was like
rushing waters, powerful and soothing at the same time.

The minute He said, "I am the truth," I knew immediately it
was Jesus. He didn't say, "I am Jesus," but every fiber of my being
knew who He was. I had never read the Bible before, but somehow
I knew what Jesus was saying to me was in the Bible. I was so

consumed by His presence that I dropped to my knees and looked up at Him. He is so glorious, so beautiful. All light inside of Light.

I said, "Lord! You are Lord!" He said, "Yes, I am Jesus, the One you denied. The One you said is not the Son of God. I came to save you, to make you a happy person. You don't have to do anything, just know that I love you." I said, "That's it?" He said, "Yes, believe in Me." It was like I went to school and studied everything in one day. All of a sudden Jesus made sense to me. . . .

He got so close that there was too much light to even see the color of His eyes. It was not like looking at any human being. Somehow with His being and His voice came light. A huge light. An overwhelming light. He was talking to me, but at the same time I was seeing Heaven right before my eyes. . . . He didn't preach to me; He was just talking to me like another person, but with a beautiful and strong voice. It was loving, and sweet like honey.[1]

This is a beautiful story of how God is found by those who seek him. For this Muslim woman, reporting such a vision carried risk of severe persecution, yet the assurance she had of Jesus's love and light filled her with confidence to share boldly.

God wants all people to know him intimately! He revealed himself through Jesus so we could know him in a personal and relatable way. God wants you to know you are loved and eternally safe because of what Jesus did on the cross, suffering and dying in your place, so you can be reconciled to God. And this amazing grace is available to all people willing to receive it.

Jesus is the way, the truth, and the life. He wants you to experience the depth of love he feels for you. In gratitude, be ready to share his love with others who have not heard of Jesus, so they too can experience the joy of his salvation offered to all people.

Prayer: *Dear Jesus, thank you for opening the way to God through your life, death, and resurrection. Help me to be bold enough to share the good news with people in my life who don't know you.*

78

> I saw the dead . . . standing before God's throne. And the books were opened, including the Book of Life. And the dead were judged according to what they had done, as recorded in the books.
>
> Revelation 20:12 NLT

DEREK PROFESSED FAITH in Christ at age nine, but by thirteen he wanted to go a different path. For twenty-five years he made a fortune with drugs and crime. It all came to a crashing halt when he had a near-fatal car accident.

My first thoughts were about how and when my family would find out that I had died, and how would my dog be fed and taken care of. Then it got more serious, as I realized that it did not matter whether I was wealthy or poor, or whether I was driving a luxury car or a junker, because I was about to leave this earth. I did not feel qualified to pray for my life at that time. However, I had a one-way conversation with God, and I acknowledged to him that my life had been one of foolishness. I told Him that I no longer had the strength to live, and if I was to do so, it would take his direct intervention. . . . [F]or the first time in my life, I had peace and was grateful that dying wasn't all that bad. . . .

I was taken up into a large area where I could not see anyone else but could sense life around me. . . . I was then "brought" up to a large table that had a very large book on it that was open, but was placed in such a manner so that it could be read only by someone on the other side whom I could not see. I knew that this had to be the Book of Life that I had heard about as a youth, and that if my name did not appear in it I would have to go to hell. This was very serious indeed, but as I stood there, the book closed. That did not seem to be a very good sign. . . . I had had plenty of opportunities to change, but now it was too late. . . .

Before any sort of trap door opened up to send me to hell, I was taken to a second table, just like the first one, except this book was closed. I was somewhat confused as to what this second book was all about, when suddenly it opened up and this scene was a repetition of the first scene. This entire second book made no sense at all as I had only heard of one book. . . . Then all of a sudden, my name was found in the second book, and I thought to myself, "Great, I get to go to heaven."[1]

Derek miraculously recovered and later learned about the two books he experienced. Revelation 20 says the Book of Life records those who recognize their need for God's saving grace and forgiveness offered in Christ. But God is also recording all our thoughts and deeds in books from which he wants to reward us (Revelation 20:12, Psalm 56:8). Derek reflects:

> God had shown me that I was acceptable to him through my confession as a young child, but my works were not acceptable . . . and for this reason he sent me back, so that when this scene is repeated, something may be stated for my benefit.[2]

If you've accepted God's gift of forgiveness and adoption offered freely because of Jesus's payment on your behalf, your name is in the Book of Life, securing your place in Heaven. As Romans 8:38 affirms, nothing can separate you from God's love!

God also keeps track of our good deeds and wants to reward you with eternal treasures for every pure motive and act of kindness. Perhaps he has our angels recording our deeds, so that all of God's creatures learn the lessons of earth (see Mal. 3:16). Every little deed done out of love for God, using your gifts to serve people, is building for you an eternal reward. Let that motivate how you face every challenge and opportunity today.

Prayer: *Dear Lord, I am so grateful for my salvation, and I want to show my love for you through my acts of kindness and deeds done to bless others.*

79

I have loved you with an everlasting love; I have drawn you
with unfailing kindness.

Jeremiah 31:3

GOD LOVES YOU MORE than you can imagine! Hazeliene
from Singapore discovered experientially the truth of this
statement when she blacked out, hit her head, and apparently "died." She explains in English (not her native language):

I suddenly was in the very dark tunnel going up, up, up. . . . After
passing through from that very dark tunnel, it has changed to very
bright light. I had seen a very bright light, I thought it was sun,
but it was not. I don't have an idea where that light came from.

Someone spoke to me for a while, I heard, and that voice came
from that light. You know what I felt when I saw that light? When
I saw that bright light, I felt that someone loves me very much (but
no idea who it was). I was very overwhelmed with that bright light.

And while I was there, I felt the love, and that love I never felt
before. That light welcoming me very warmly and loves me very
much. My words to the light before I [revived] was this: I wanted
to stay here, but I love my two kids. When I said this, I suddenly
woke up. . . .

Was it true that the light was GOD? Reason why I felt very
overwhelmed? I felt that only that light ever love me and no one
does. All people know only to beat me, hurt me, criticized me,
offended me and many more. Nobody love me like that kind of
love before. How I wish my two kids and me could go there and
feel that love forever.[1]

Dr. Mary Neal shares how personal God's love is for each of us:

God knows each and every one of us individually, created each
and every one of us individually, loves each and every one of us as

though we are the only ones, and has a plan for each and every one of our lives that's one of beauty. And, for me, that was profound because I never understood that. There are billions. How can it happen? And I can't explain how it can be true, but it is.[2]

It is amazing to think about the Creator of the universe loving each of us individually and personally as if you or I were the only person on earth. But it is true—he loves you like that, and nothing can be compared to the intensity and magnitude of the love of your Heavenly Father.

This may be difficult to understand, especially if your earthly parents did not demonstrate an extravagant love toward you. But God is a perfect Father, and he does love you like that—in fact, he *is* love. He wants you to live in his love every day of your life, as his loving-kindness continuously draws you closer to him.

Today, focus on how much he loves you and all the ways he's been kind to you. You are unconditionally loved as if you were the only one God loves. Let this fill you up and reassure you of your worth to him as his beloved child.

Prayer: *Lord Jesus, thank you for loving me so faithfully and completely. Help me draw near to you today as I meditate on your everlasting love and unfailing kindness toward me, your child.*

80

How long, LORD? Will you forget me forever? How long will you hide your face from me? How long must I wrestle with my thoughts and day after day have sorrow in my heart? How long will my enemy triumph over me? Look on me and answer, LORD my God. . . . But I trust in your unfailing love; my heart rejoices in your salvation.

Psalm 13:1–3, 5

SEVERAL PEOPLE describe the perfect understanding they experienced in God's presence during their NDEs, which can give us hope to patiently endure when our questions go unanswered today. When Jeff's car rolled multiple times, he found himself in a different place. He shares:

[I was the] same as I had always been, only now bathed in this familiar and amazing light. My natural senses were magnified to a greater degree. There were a million questions racing through my head, but as soon as I thought of a question, the answer was immediately there.[1]

Hafur, a woman from Colombia, recalls,

I understood everything with a great clarity and super-lucidity I had never experienced before. I realized I had wasted time in suffering, and what I should have been doing was using my freedom to choose true love, and not pain, in all that came into my life.[2]

Crystal McVea had been through many tribulations and always thought:

"If I ever meet [God], I'm going to ask Him . . . How could He allow such evil to exist in the world?" Why, I would ask Him, was he such a punishing God? But in heaven, all those questions immediately evaporated. In His presence, I absolutely understood that in every way God's plan is perfect. . . . Does that mean I can now explain [evil and suffering]? No. I understood it in heaven, but we aren't meant to have that kind of understanding here on Earth. All I can tell you is that I know God's plan is perfect. In His radiance, it all makes perfect, perfect sense. In this way all the questions I had for God were answered without me even having to ask them.

And yet, standing in His glorious presence, filled with His infinite wisdom, there was still one question I felt compelled to ask . . . "Why? Why didn't I do more for You? Why didn't I accomplish more in Your name? Why didn't I talk more about You? Why didn't I do what You asked me to do?" It's not that I felt regret—it's that I loved God so immensely I felt like He deserved so much more from me. But God wouldn't allow me to feel bad about it. There is no feeling bad in heaven. . . . He is a loving God. I realized I didn't just love God. I realized He IS love.[3]

Sometimes in life it feels like God is hiding, like we are getting attacked by enemies and God is doing nothing. Even King David, a man after God's own heart, felt this way as he penned the words of Psalm 13 quoted above. God wants you to bring your pain to him as you struggle with the evils of life. Just as David did, you can talk honestly to God about what you are going through.

Your Heavenly Father has compassion on you and doesn't want you to feel alone. He will take you through your hardship to the other side, and there will be a day when all your questions will find answers. As the apostle Paul encouraged, a day is coming when you "will know everything completely, just as God now knows [you] completely" (1 Cor. 13:12 NLT). Until then, you can find strength as King David did, trusting in the unfailing love of God. Your salvation in Christ will bring you peace amidst the sorrow.

> **Prayer:** *Dear Lord, as I persevere during life's hardships and trials, I will trust in your unfailing love and rejoice in my salvation, knowing you will lead me through to the other side.*

81

Go and enjoy choice food and sweet drinks, and send some to those who have nothing prepared. This day is holy to our Lord. Do not grieve, for the joy of the LORD is your strength.

Nehemiah 8:10

HEAVEN WILL BE a thriving, joyful, festive place, where families and friends work together and then gather for feasts and parties to celebrate and enjoy life with the Giver of Life. It will give God great joy as we enjoy him together in his Holy City.

Linda went through a life review and then, as she recalls it,

All these people showed up—hundreds of them, as though they were having a party and they knew me and I knew them . . . they showed me a city. A big city. It had golden colors, and there was this big explosion coming up over the city of lights and rainbows and colors that we don't have here, that we can't even explain. Those colors would hurt our eyes if we looked at them. But not there. It was glorious.[1]

A woman who had a heart attack reported:

I went to a place that was beautifully lit—like the sunshine but much prettier and more golden. . . . [It] seemed like a neighborhood, and I was shown around to all the people I loved and missed, and they were all so happy.[2]

Maybe you never thought about Heaven's neighborhoods and celebrations, but God enjoys us enjoying him and each other. The Old Testament prophets looked forward to Heaven's feasts.

[The LORD] will spread a wonderful feast for all the people of the world. It will be a delicious banquet with clear, well-aged wine and choice meat. There he will remove the cloud of gloom, the shadow of death that hangs over the earth. He will swallow up death forever! (Isa. 25:6–8 NLT)

At the Last Supper, the night before his crucifixion, "[Jesus] took a cup of wine and gave thanks to God for it. Then he said, 'Take this and share it among yourselves. For I will not drink wine again until the Kingdom of God has come. . . . [And you will] eat and drink at my table in my Kingdom'" (Luke 22:17–18, 30 NLT). The City of God will be filled with celebration, and God himself will be at the center of it all!

What an amazing thought—that all who live to serve the King while on this earth will one day experience the King serving us. In Luke 12:37 Jesus tells us, "The servants who are ready and waiting for [the King's] return will be rewarded. I tell you the truth, he [Jesus] himself will seat them, put on an apron, and serve them as they sit and eat!" (NLT).

Heaven will be a joyous celebration of God! All the festivities of earth—the cultural creativity, learning, exploration, and celebrations—are merely a foretaste of Heaven.

Yes, we can abuse what God intended for good (like getting drunk with wine), but he has given us many things to enjoy in his presence and in line with his will, now and forever. Just think about how all your joy and laughter, celebrations and parties with friends and family, when done in acknowledgment of God's goodness delights the Lord! This is why God commanded Israel to celebrate before him three times a year in Jerusalem.

This week, as you enjoy the company of friends and family, thank God for them, and enjoy him as you enjoy each other. As Nehemiah said, let the joy of the Lord give you strength.

Prayer: *Thank you, Lord, that every good gift comes from you, including joyous celebration. Help me to enjoy my friends and family in gratitude to you, and let your joy be my strength!*

82

> I saw a throne in heaven and someone sitting on it. The one
> sitting on the throne was as brilliant as gemstones—like
> jasper and carnelian. And the glow of an emerald circled
> his throne like a rainbow.
>
> Revelation 4:2–3

IN THE CENTER of the City of God is the architectural wonder of the universe, amazing not just for its physical beauty, but for the mystery, wonder, and awe created by the very presence of the Father, Son, and Holy Spirit. There is no place imaginable you would rather be than the throne of God.

The throne is more than what we often picture in our minds. It is a place encompassing the heart of Heaven and the center of the most spectacular displays of human art, worship, dance, creativity—all presented to the greatest Being in existence and celebrated before all humanity to glorify God.

Here are accounts of several people who describe the splendor of God's throne from different perspectives:

> [I] could see the throne, dazzling, brilliant white—it's hard to imagine in this dark world, but there my eyes could see so much clearer so much farther away. I saw huge white pillars surrounding the throne, and an enormous crowd of people, men and women, boys and girls, dancing and singing along in a mass choir of praise to the two Beings seated on it.[1]

> Everything in heaven flowed into and out of the Throne. It pulsed like a dynamo. . . . The Throne Building was huge—beyond my ability to understand . . . several hundred miles wide and at least fifty miles tall, and it had a domed roof. . . . Thousands of steps led up to the Throne. . . . As we began to go up the stairway, I saw hundreds of

thousands or perhaps millions of people going into and coming out from the Throne. They were worshipping and praising God. . . .

The entry area, or gateway, had columns. . . . The Throne was made out of some heavenly material. It was crystal clear, yet it consisted of what appeared to be gold and ivory and silver. . . . [It] was the most beautiful spot in heaven.[2]

[The Throne Room] was wider and higher than I could even imagine—hundreds of miles, with massive arches and pillars. . . . I could feel a difference as I approached the throne. As I got near to it, the air became electrically charged with the power and presence of God. . . . God is so intently God that I couldn't go easily before him—I thought I would vaporize . . . the closer I got to the throne, the more everything became transparent. Everything is absolutely transparent, with purity closest to God.[3]

In front of the throne is a large oval area . . . made out of sapphire jewels. I found this also in Ezekiel [1:22–28], describing the sapphires underneath the throne of God and it's called a sea because it's blue and because it's shiny. It's called glass because it's actually made of sapphires that represent glass, so that's the term "sea of glass." In other words it's not water; it's not the flowing of the Spirit of God, it's a rather solid place to stand.[4]

If we could see God on his throne, we'd never want to leave his presence. The power, glory, and grandeur of God far exceeds anything you could ever want or dream of in this life. God is magnificent, terrifying power and the essence of pure, unconditional love, all at the same time. We will worship him out of sheer awe and wonder—in community with all of our family in Heaven.

Imagine being in God's presence, and take time to worship him today. It shows love and honor to God as you recognize how mighty and majestic he is.

Prayer: *Lord, I worship you in your splendor and majesty, and I recognize you are the Creator over all things great and small. Thank you for your power in my life.*

83

Three things will last forever—faith, hope, and love—and the greatest of these is love.

1 Corinthians 13:13 NLT

HOWARD, BY NATURE, is very candid and expressive about his NDE. In an interview, he shared about the face-to-face conversation he had with Jesus, and the importance of loving others:

I'll tell you what Jesus told me to do because I asked him that exact question: "If I come back into this world, what would be my purpose?"

And before he had a chance to answer, I said, "You know, I'm an artist. I'm going to build you a huge shrine." And he said, "Please don't do that." And I was like, "But I'm an artist. That's what I do, you know? It will be great. . . . It will be wonderful. People will come from all over the world." And he said, "I don't need it." And I was, "What do you mean you don't need it? There are all kinds of shrines and cathedrals built to you." He said, "Yeah, well . . . they're not for me. They're for people."

He said, "I have a purpose for you. . . . Your purpose is to love the person that you're with." And I said, "Yeah, okay, great. I got that. What do you want me to do?" And he said, "No, that's it." And I said, "That's it?! Love the person I am with?" And he said, "That's your whole purpose." And I said, "What good will that do?" And he said, "It will change the whole world."

I said, "Come on, there's billions of people in the world. How in the world would me loving someone change the world?" . . . He laughed and he said, "If you love the person that you're with, they'll love the person that they're with and they'll love the person that they're with. And that will multiply." And I said, "Yeah, but what if somebody gets hit by a truck or gets sick or something? Then it all falls apart." And he said, "You're not the only one." And I said, "Who else is involved in this plan?" He said, "Well, there are millions all over the world in the love plan," and I said, "Yeah, but there's billions of people. It's not enough. You need more." And he said, "There's billions more." And I said, "Who's that?" And he said, "The angels." And I said, "Well, *that* might do it!"

And he said, "There's one more." And I said, "Who is that?" And he said, "God. It's God's plan. It's going to work." He said, "Whether you believe it or not, whether you like it or not, it's God's plan. It *will* work. Just love the person that you're with."

So, that's what I've been struggling with for 30 years. Trying to do that. It's not as easy as it sounds. As a matter of fact, it's the most interesting challenge I have ever had . . . he should have told me to become a brain surgeon or a rocket scientist, because that would have been a whole lot easier than what I'm trying to do.[1]

Love is the essence of who God is, and the most important thing we can do. As Scripture says, the greatest virtue we can possess the ability to love others as God does. His love is powerful and will produce positive effects for eternity.

When you love another human being, you are acting on what is the center of the heart of God. His love has power to change hearts and redeem lives. His love covers sins and conquers evil (see 1 Peter 4:8). As a believer, you can participate in his transformational work by loving others in your path and letting God's power work through you, even when you encounter hard-to-love people. This is when God's supernatural love can shine the most!

Today, receive the power of love from the One who is Love, and give it to others in your life. No matter how difficult or impossible it may seem, he will show you ways to love beyond your ability, if you are willing.

Prayer: *Thank you, God, for loving me unconditionally, and help me to generously pour your love out to others you put in my life.*

84

Now if we are children, then we are heirs—heirs of God and co-heirs with Christ, if indeed we share in his sufferings in order that we may also share in his glory.

Romans 8:17

HAVE YOU EVER WONDERED what it means to share in God's glory? Dr. Mary Neal confirms the brilliant glory radiating from the people she called her welcoming committee:

They were radiating a brilliance that was indescribable. It was as though they were like the Northern Lights in that they were of a physical form, but their edges were a little indistinct. It's sort of translucent, pearlescent, shimmery. A brilliance of light—just exploding in it, and the light was not just something you would see. If you look at the sun, you see light and it's blinding. This was really a light born out of love. I don't know quite how else to explain it.[1]

Rebecca, a woman from the 1890s, noticed, "The material out of which my robe was fashioned was unlike anything that I had ever seen. It was soft and light and shone with a faint luster."[2]

A man from New Zealand describes the glory he witnessed:

[Jesus's] garments were not man-made fabrics but were like garments of light. As I lifted my eyes up I could see the chest of a man with his arms outstretched as if to welcome me. I looked towards his face. It was so bright; it seemed to be about ten times brighter than the light I'd already seen. It made the sun look yellow and pale in comparison. It was so bright that I couldn't make out the features of his face, and as I stood there I began to sense that the light was emitting purity and holiness. I knew that I was standing in the presence of Almighty God.[3]

Rene from Australia shares that when she saw Jesus, she "became fascinated by the fabric of His robe, trying to figure out how light could be woven."[4]

When Jesus was on earth, he took Peter, James, and John alone with him and they saw him transfigured in glory. Scripture says, "The appearance of his face changed, and his clothes became as bright as a flash of lightning. Two men, Moses and Elijah, appeared in glorious splendor, talking with Jesus" (Luke 9:29–30). When Jesus lets these three disciples see his glory, he and these two Old Testament prophets are clothed in brilliant light. So glory and light seem to go together; but as NDErs attest, they come out of a person in palpable ways.

On earth, we enjoy dressing in a way that shows our best attributes and style. What if in Heaven we are most proud of the extent to which the light and glory of God shines through us? Though NDErs say they saw people wear ordinary clothes in Heaven, many wear robes of white (see Rev. 3:5) that seem to allow God's glory to shine through. The glory of God is light, love, and life, all woven together, shining out of believers who have allowed him to shine through them.

Radiating the light and love of God sourced from within us will be the most exhilarating feeling. Imagine what it feels like to experience God's light and love filling you from the inside—shining out of you in glorious brilliance!

Live today radiating his glory as you encounter people in your path, and shine his love and life on others who need his presence. "Those who are wise will shine like the brightness of the heavens, and those who lead many to righteousness, like the stars for ever and ever" (Dan. 12:3).

Prayer: *Lord Jesus, I want to shine your light and love in all I do. Help me to radiate your glory through my thoughts, words, and actions.*

85

> Since the children have flesh and blood, he too shared in their humanity. . . . For this reason he had to be made like them, fully human in every way, in order that he might become a merciful and faithful high priest in service to God, and that he might make atonement for the sins of the people.
>
> Hebrews 2:14, 17

JESUS UNDERSTANDS US more than we can ever imagine. In fact, it shocks people to realize that he not only knows our languages but even our colloquialisms. When Samaa decided to return, Jesus said colloquially in her native tongue, "Okay, see ya soon."[1]

Similarly, Khalida found him speaking to her in Arabic in a conversational way:

> He didn't preach to me; He was just talking to me like another person, but with a beautiful and strong voice. . . . I also knew that He is a Father and I was His daughter and His chosen one. All the pain in my life He already knew about, and He was already pleased with me. I knew that all is forgiven by the blood of Jesus. . . . I was begging Him not to leave me there. "I need You," I told Him, not wanting to ever be without Him again. He said to me in Arabic, "I'm going to come back and get you."[2]

Vicki had been blind from birth, yet as part of her life review Jesus showed her a scene where, in a fit of jealousy, Vicki had ripped the buttons and lace off the fancy dress of another blind classmate.

> Vicki: It was like, you know, I could feel from Jesus [his] understanding and compassion about how I felt that way, and why I did it. But, you know, it was sort of like he talked to me during that time. He says, "Yeah, that wasn't too cool."

Interviewer: Really? You're not kidding me?

Vicki: No. That's exactly what he said.[3]

Derry had a near-fatal automobile accident. During her NDE she recognized Jesus:

> As I walked with this heavenly personage, his countenance shone forth with such a brightness that I can't describe. I knew this heavenly personage was Jesus because I recognized him as a familiar friend. He didn't announce who he was because this wasn't necessary. I remember walking with Jesus, but we weren't walking in the physical sense, the best way I can describe our walking was that we were walking in mid-air, floating above the ground of this beautiful garden.[4]

Sometimes it is hard to truly comprehend how Jesus can be fully human and divine. Having lived as a human on earth, Jesus experienced emotions, temptations, physical pain, joys, sadness, celebrations, and disappointments just as you do. He truly understands your every feeling and wants to draw near to you as your closest friend.

The intimacy of the love God has for us is hard to comprehend. The only comparison comes by analogy: the connection you feel with a best friend, the bond you feel with a parent, the oneness you experience with a spouse, your tender care and concern for your children. Yet these all fall short, because nothing can fully compare to the intimacy and bond you will feel with Jesus.

Think about Jesus as your best friend and confidant, always available to you, always kind and compassionate. Jesus is a person who will never fail you nor forsake you. Find comfort in his friendship today!

Prayer: *Dear Jesus, thank you for humbling yourself to become human and desiring an intimate relationship with me. I am so grateful to call you friend.*

86

We know that when this earthly tent we live in is taken down
. . . we will have a house in heaven, an eternal body made for
us by God himself and not by human hands.

2 Corinthians 5:1 NLT

D<small>R. RICHARD EBY AND HIS WIFE</small> were helping clean out a relative's Chicago apartment. Richard leaned against a second-story railing to drop boxes down. He did not know termites had destroyed the wood anchoring the railing, and it gave way. Richard plunged two stories to the cement sidewalk below—headfirst! He recalls, "I was dead on impact."

Richard miraculously revived in the morgue, but while "dead," he noticed:

> I was the same size, the same shape, as the person I had seen in the mirror for years. I was clothed in a translucent flowing gown, pure white, but transparent to my gaze. In amazement I could see through my body and note the gorgeously white flowers behind and beneath me. This seemed perfectly normal, yet thrillingly novel. . . .
>
> My feet were easy to see. No bifocals needed. I had instantly noted that my eyes were unlimited in range of vision; ten inches or ten miles—the focus was sharp and clear. . . . There were no bones or vessels or organs. No blood. Again my mind which worked here in Heaven with electric-like speed answered my unspoken query: they are not needed; Jesus is the Life here. He is the needed energy. . . .[1]

Richard also noticed his new spiritual body offered amazing possibilities:

> There is nothing in the physics of Heaven that's similar to the physics on earth. . . . If I asked a question, He had the answer

ready before I even asked it. Jesus and I walked in Heaven together, but it was more like flying than walking. We were talking while suspended in midair.[2]

It is mind-boggling to comprehend the scope of what we will experience living in our new bodies in Heaven! One thing's for sure: you will be perfect, and your Heavenly body will run on the energy from God himself.

"The body that is sown is perishable, it is raised imperishable; it is sown in dishonor, it is raised in glory; it is sown in weakness, it is raised in power; it is sown a natural body, it is raised a spiritual body" (1 Cor. 15:42–44). Never again will you have to manage or cope with a compromised, broken, or flawed body in any way, shape, or form. This seems too good to be true, but it is your reality as a believer.

Today, even though you may face challenges and physical hardship in your life, find comfort in knowing that they will one day come to an end. On that day you will have a new and improved body that is everything you ever dreamed and more, and this body will last forever.

> **Prayer**: *Heavenly Father, as I live in this earthly body that is flawed and blemished, help me to focus on what is to come. Thank you that I will be energetic, healthy, and vibrant with you as the source of my strength forever.*

87

I pray also for those who will believe in me through their
message, that all of them may be one, Father, just as you are
in me and I am in you. May they also be in us so that the
world may believe that you have sent me.

John 17:20–21

WITH PERFECT COMMUNICATION and perfect love comes perfect unity. Captain Dale Black describes it like this:

The best unity I have ever felt on earth did not compare with the
exhilarating oneness that I experienced with my spiritual family in
heaven. This love . . . God's love, was transforming. To experience
something so sacred, so profound as the boundless love of God
was the most thrilling part of heaven.

Somehow I knew that light and life and love were connected
and interrelated. It was as if the very heart of God lay open for
everyone in heaven to bask in its glory, to warm themselves in its
presence, to bathe in its almost liquid properties so they could be
restored, renewed, refreshed. Remarkably, the light didn't shine on
things but through them. . . .

I recognized that Jesus, the Word, was the structure that held it
all together. Like the rib cage around the heart. He was the creative
power that brought everything that I saw into place and stabilized
it. The multitudes of angels and people were responding to the will
of God and acting in perfect order to accomplish His will. Even
light—the way it traveled and reflected—was highly complex, yet
mathematical and precise. The melodies and rhythms of the music
were all in perfect order. Nothing out of sync. No part of heaven
was independent of the whole. There was complete unity.[1]

Eben Alexander describes this mysterious unity in his NDE:
"Everything was distinct," he remembers, "yet everything was also
a part of everything else." He recalls that hearing and seeing were

not separate there. He could somehow hear the visual beauty of the angels above his head and see the "surging, joyful perfection" of their songs. He felt he was actually melding with the sounds and sights, somehow mysteriously uniting or joining together with them.[2]

Another NDEr describes God's unifying light like electricity:

> Every being there has God the Father and Jesus inside of them. They live outside of every being and inside every being. Every being shines because of the Father and Jesus. They are the light within every living being and creature.[3]

Dean likens this unifying power to our electricity:

> One of the most fascinating things I experienced was being connected to everything there at the same moment. It is like the electricity that connects power to run anything that needs electric energy here. It is like our computer system that is connected to the Internet, which connects us to every computer in the world. God connects every one of His creations together.[4]

Jesus's last prayer was for our unity, that we would bring Heaven to earth by letting his kingdom come, his will be done, as one body representing Jesus together. Yet so often this is hard to do.

Our unity in Christ is a threat to Satan, and the evil one will do all he can to divide us. Even so, Scripture says, "as far as it depends on you, live at peace with everyone" (Rom. 12:18). This will stretch you and grow you into becoming more like Jesus. Where there is strife, be a peacemaker. Where there is hurt, be a healer. Where there is conflict, be a reconciler.

Today, focus on how you can be an answer to Jesus's prayer, "that they may be one just as we are one" (John 17:11). The evil one will have no power against unified believers in Christ!

> **Prayer:** Lord, help me to love my brothers and sisters in Christ and to strive today for the unity we will have in Heaven.

88

For we do not have a high priest who is unable to empathize with our weaknesses, but we have one who has been tempted in every way, just as we are—yet he did not sin. Let us then approach God's throne of grace with confidence, so that we may receive mercy and find grace to help us in our time of need.

Hebrews 4:15–16

DURING GEORGE RITCHIE'S ENCOUNTER with Jesus, he discovered that the Lord knew everything about him.

When I say He knew everything about me, this was simply an observable fact. For into that room along with His radiant presence—simultaneously, though in telling about it I have to describe them one by one—had also entered every single episode of my entire life. Everything that had ever happened to me was simply there, in full view, contemporary and current, all seemingly taking place at that moment.

How this was possible I did not know. . . .

Transfixed, I stared at myself standing at the blackboard in a third-grade spelling class. Receiving my Eagle badge in front of my scout troop. Wheeling Papa Dabney onto the verandah at Moss Side. . . .

There were other scenes, hundreds, thousands, all illuminated by that searing Light, in an existence where time seemed to have ceased. It would have taken weeks of ordinary time. . . .

Every detail of twenty years of living was there to be looked at. . . .

What have you done with your life to show Me? . . .

Have you loved others as I am loving you? Totally? Unconditionally? . . .

Why, I had not known love like this was possible. Someone should have told me, I thought indignantly! A fine time to discover what life was all about. . . .

I did tell you.

But how? Still wanting to justify myself. How could He have told me and I not have heard?

I told you by the life I lived. I told you by the death I died. And, if you keep your eyes on Me, you will see more. . . .

From that loneliest moment of my existence [facing death] I had leaped into the most perfect belonging I had ever known. The Light of Jesus had entered my life and filled it completely, and the idea of being separated from Him was more than I could bear.[1]

After this life-altering encounter, George made it to medical school, worked for thirteen years as a medical doctor, and eventually formed what would be the precursor to the Peace Corps.

Even though God knows everything we have ever done, thought, or will do, both good and bad, we are still completely and totally loved and accepted by him.

You can take your temptations, regrets, and struggles to Jesus, because he is our high priest who empathizes and understands. He was tempted in every way we are tempted. He knows your faults and still loves you more than you can imagine. He wants to lead and guide you to live the life he has intended for you—one of purpose and fulfillment—so confidently go to him when you're struggling. You will find grace in your time of need.

Today, think about how much God loves you, just as you are. Let him into your mind and thoughts to transform you into more of the person he created you to be.

Prayer: *Lord, thank you for loving me and accepting me despite my shortcomings. I want to align myself to your thoughts and actions today and become more of the person you made me to be.*

89

The heavens declare the glory of God; the skies proclaim
the work of his hands.

Psalm 19:1

MARV FOUND HIMSELF CAPTIVATED as the atmosphere of
Heaven projected a glorious light show, displayed on the
most brilliant shades of deep blue sky as the backdrop:

The sky in which I flew to heaven, and the firmament surrounding
the heavens, were a wilder and bluer yonder than you would ever
believe. . . . The closest shade I can associate this otherworldly blue
with is the surreal tones of the water in the Caribbean or off the
coast of Hawaii at sunset. . . . That color is waiting for you and
me on the other side. . . .

The colors and lights in heaven were simply sublime. . . . They
were the deepest, richest, most gloriously lush colors I had ever
seen, and some I had never seen before. Heaven is a dream-come-
true for those who love all things colorful, and our home there is
lit by the Father of Lights. . . . The white in heaven was like none
other I can compare. From a brilliant white to an opal stone to a
milk glass moon color, the white shades clustered in the sky like a
huge bridal bouquet. . . .

The colors in heaven would meld from whites into blues and reds
and purples and greens. The multiple colors would change and shift
and move constantly, twirling and twisting and floating . . . shape-
shifting in a way that fixated and enthralled me. The closest I can
come to describing what that light show was like is probably the
aurora borealis, or the northern lights. . . . Then again, if I compare
the light show in Alaska to the light show in heaven . . . it's not even
close. . . . Even just the light show was utterly transfixing.[1]

Marv then noticed the lush landscape of Heaven:

Picture the verdant, luscious grass at the Masters [golf tournament] and then try to imagine grass far greener and more deluxe. That's how green the grass is in heaven.[2]

About sixty yards away, in the middle left of the panorama before me, were some old fishing boats pulled up on the shore of a huge, rippling lake. The boats looked worn and aged, not sleek and razzy dazzy like the boats we see zooming around on Lake Michigan. . . . They lay on a sandy, rocky seashore. The blue of the lake was a darker, less brilliant blue than the shade of heaven's sky, and the surface had a few gentle waves. Like an ocean or one of the Great Lakes, I couldn't see the other side.[3]

Imagine these surreal colors and beautiful imagery described above. How awesome it is to realize that we are made in the image of this magnificently brilliant, creative God! Every created thing reflects his glory.

As he displays his artistry and creative abilities in all colors, shapes, and forms, we as his creatures have creative gifts he wants us to express to reflect his image. Sometimes we are reluctant to explore them, because we think we might fail or not really have it in us like we see others expressing. However, the truth is, we are created to reflect him in all his beauty and color, no one of us exactly like the other. We just need to unleash this potential and let him develop the gifts he has already blessed us with.

Today, ask God to reveal to you the talents you have that reflect his colorful and diverse creativity. This doesn't have to be in the ways you normally would think, either. It could be in the way you cook, plan activities for your children, or even design spreadsheets. Dream about how you reflect his glory.

Prayer: *Heavenly Father, thank you that I am made in your image. Help me to see your creativity and artistry in creation and in myself, and to reflect your creativity back to the world.*

90

"I thought to myself, 'I would love to treat you as my own children!' I wanted nothing more than to give you this beautiful land—the finest possession in the world. I looked forward to your calling me 'Father,' and I wanted you never to turn from me. But you have been unfaithful to me, you people of Israel! . . . My wayward children," says the LORD, "come back to me, and I will heal your wayward hearts."

Jeremiah 3:19–20, 22 NLT

THE GOD OF THE BIBLE is an emotional Being. He longs for a loving relationship with those he created. He uses every human relational metaphor to describe how he feels about us.

As a university professor, Howard Storm lived most of his life denying God, yet he cried out to Jesus during his NDE. Jesus rescued him and held him as they watched his life review:

There was a number of angels who had been recording my entire life all my life and Jesus wanted them to play out, in chronological order, the scenes of my life. And the entire emphasis was on my interaction with other people. As my life progressed, my adolescence into adulthood, I saw myself turning completely away from God, church, all that, and becoming a person who decided that life was all about the biggest, baddest bear in the woods wins.

And now I began to experience Jesus's and the angels' literal pain. Emotional pain with watching the sins in my life. And here's the nicest, kindest, most loving being I've ever met who, I realized, is my Lord, my Savior, even my Creator, holding me and supporting me, trying to give me more understanding of my life. And it was figuratively—not literally—like I was stabbing him in the heart as we're watching this stuff. And the last thing I want to do is to hurt him, and I don't want to hurt him to this day. Jesus is a very feeling man. God is a very feeling creator.[1]

Another NDEr describes God's light coming through him like powerful waves of emotion:

> The first wave of light gave off an amazing warmth and comfort. It was as though the light wasn't just material in nature but was a "living light" that transmitted an emotion. The light passed into me and filled me with a sense of love and acceptance. Halfway down another wave of light passed into me. This light gave off total and complete peace. . . . A third wave broke off the main source of light as I neared the end of the tunnel. This wave hit me and as it did total joy went through my being. It was so exciting that I knew that what I was about to see would be the most awesome experience in all my life.[2]

God is our Heavenly Father. He has emotions to express just like we have. He is filled with joy when his children love and follow him, and he is filled with sadness when we reject his loving guidance and are unfaithful to him. He created you to know him in a personal, intimate way. He delights in you, and he always understands what you are going through. He longs to give you good gifts and pour his love and peace into your heart and mind.

He laughs with you in your joys and cries with you in your pain. It hurts him when we hurt ourselves or others by turning from his will and ways, yet it brings him great joy when we do his will and treat people as he would: "Whatever you did for one of the least of these brothers and sisters of mine, you did for me" (Matt. 25:40).

He is the most loving Father or parent you could ever have, now and forever. Today, meditate on a personal attribute of God that specifically encourages you, and feel how his love fills your heart.

> **Prayer:** *Dear God, thank you that you are an emotional and expressive God, and that you delight in me. Please help me to bring you joy as I reflect your love to those around me today.*

91

> They broke bread in their homes and ate together with glad and sincere hearts, praising God and enjoying the favor of all the people.
>
> Acts 2:46–47

IMAGINE YOUR DREAM HOUSE—in your dream location. So many people strive and sacrifice and save to get the perfect retirement home in the perfect place.

In a fascinating near-death experience written in 1898, Rebecca Springer reported what other Christians who were revived would report a hundred years later about the homes of Heaven. Rebecca died of a high fever and traveled to a place where she found

> the softest and most beautiful turf of grass, thickly studded with fragrant flowers, many of them the flowers I had known and loved on earth . . . others of like nature wholly unfamiliar to me. . . .
>
> Away, away—far beyond the limit of my vision, I well knew [with telescopic vision]—stretched this wonderful sward of perfect grass and flowers; and out of it grew equally wonderful trees. . . . I saw, half hidden by the trees, elegant and beautiful houses of strangely attractive architecture, that I felt must be the homes of the happy inhabitants of this enchanted place.
>
> I caught glimpses of sparkling fountains in many directions, and close to my retreat flowed a river, clear as crystal . . . and instead of sunlight there was a golden and rosy glory everywhere.[1]

As Captain Dale Black flew over the great city escorted by his two angels, he described the exquisite architecture of the homes between God's throne and the great wall:

> Between the central part of the city and the city walls were groupings of brightly colored picture-perfect homes in small, quaint

towns. . . . The dwellings in these townships were not arranged in a uniform or symmetrical manner but appeared perfectly balanced somehow. Each home was customized and unique from the others yet blended harmoniously. Some were three or four stories, some were even higher. There were no two the same. If music could become homes, it would look like these, beautifully built and perfectly balanced.[2]

From the composite picture compiled from many NDEs, there are homes in the country, homes in the mountains, homes in quaint villages, and homes in the City of God. It's all one big home, one *oikos*—the Greek word not just for a house but also the larger extended family—with many smaller family dwelling places. Imagine being "home" in every place you dwell.

It is awesome to imagine the beautiful homes with lush gardens we will inhabit in heaven. How fun it will be to entertain and enjoy our friends and family in each other's homes!

And even now we can experience the joy of hospitality with our neighbors and friends, with or without the lush gardens and fancy houses. The love and kindness we offer when we open our homes to others delights the heart of God. He works in and through our hospitality to minister to those around us, blessing us equally through the community.

No matter how large or small your home is, whether it is a mansion in the hills or a garage apartment in the suburbs, you can enjoy the company of friends and serve and love others in Jesus's name. Today, begin thinking of whom you can have over for a meal or afternoon tea, and experience the joy of creating a safe place for loving community to grow.

> **Prayer:** *Lord Jesus, help me to make my home here on earth a place where community will be experienced and where people will always feel welcomed and loved.*

92

> Get rid of all bitterness, rage, anger, harsh words, and slander, as well as all types of evil behavior. Instead, be kind to each other, tenderhearted, forgiving one another, just as God through Christ has forgiven you.
>
> Ephesians 4:31–32 NLT

George Ritchie stood in Jesus's presence as every scene from his life was replayed before him, including his secret thoughts and motives:

What emanated from this Presence was unconditional love. An astonishing love. . . . This love knew the quarrels with my stepmother, my explosive temper, the thoughts I could never control . . . and loved me just the same. . . .

I saw myself turning away when my stepmother bent over to kiss me goodnight, saw the very thought itself: *I'm not going to love this woman. My mother died. Miss Williams went away. If I love her she'll leave me, too.* I watched myself at age ten, standing at that same dining room window while Dad went to the hospital to bring home Mother and our new brother Henry, saw myself deciding before I ever saw him that I was not going to like this newcomer. . . .

Every detail of twenty years of living was there to be looked at. The good, the bad, the high points, the run-of-the-mill. And with this all-inclusive view came a question. It was implicit in every scene and, like the scenes themselves, seemed to proceed from the living Light beside me. . . .

He was not asking about accomplishments and awards. The question, like everything else proceeding from Him, had to do with love. How much have you loved with your life?[1]

The importance God puts on how we treat people was deeply felt by Howard during his life review. He explains:

I would see scenes like when Homer (a real nice art student of mine from Kentucky) came into my office to tell me about the breakup of him and his girlfriend. And I sat there at my desk, pretending to listen. In my mind, I was saying, "They don't pay you enough in this university to put up with this nonsense. I'm not here to listen to the whining of some eighteen-year-old boy about his, you know . . . romantic failures." That's what I'm thinking, and he's pouring his heart out, he's crying in my office about this girl who had broken his heart, and apparently thought I was a kind enough person to lay it out to me in the privacy of my office. And instead, I was just, "Get out of here. Leave me alone."

I saw scenes where my sister was in bed, crying, and I got up in the middle of the night and went in and put my arms around her and hugged her. And Jesus and the angels were so filled with joy that I had been willing to do that, to try and, you know, help her a little bit with her grief.

But, those were rare. The sins of my indifference . . . just seeing people as objects in order to maneuver around, through, or, you know, to shift to further my goals and my ambitions [were most].[2]

In Matthew 6:4, Jesus promised that even the unseen things we do to please God hold immense value to him and will be rewarded. He looks at the heart most, and every single act done in love matters in his eyes.

Be assured that the meal you brought to a neighbor, the hospital visits you prioritized, the kind word you spoke to the store cashier—they all matter to God. The time spent listening to a friend, the affirmation you gave your spouse, the encouragement you gave your child—they hold high value in Heaven.

When your motive is to love God by loving and serving others, it counts in God's economy. He will reward you! Today, look for ways to encourage and empower others through your words and actions.

> **Prayer:** *Lord, please show me ways to bless the people around me with kindness and love, and prioritize what is most important.*

93

> [Jesus] took the children in his arms, placed his hands on
> them, and blessed them.
>
> Mark 10:16

ANN, WHO WAS TEN WEEKS PREGNANT with her first child, was at a retreat center in the mountains for a work conference with her husband when she started showing signs of a miscarriage. She had been having a very smooth pregnancy up to this point, and they were looking forward to some time away in this scenic and peaceful place. To her surprise, she began bleeding, and it became worse after several days. She called the doctor when she got home and was instructed to stay in bed.

She had been losing enormous amounts of blood and felt extremely weak, but she lay down as told. She shares what happened next:

> When I closed my eyes, I saw the spirit of the child leaving me, and I was floating up with him. He turned to me and said telepathically that I could not come, but it was his time to leave. He thanked me for taking good care of him while he was with me and not to worry that I had done anything wrong, because I hadn't. He assured me too that he was very happy to be in Heaven and would be taken care of there.[1]

When Ann came back to consciousness, she was told by the doctor that her baby had died. Even though she already knew he had died, recovering from her miscarriage was a slow and painful process.

Many near-death experiencers speak about the babies and children they see in Heaven. Marv Besteman shares, "[I] saw babies and children and grown-ups of all ages playing and talking and laughing on grass that was the greenest green I've ever seen."[2]

Carrying a child in the womb is a sacred experience, and the impact upon the mother when the child dies before birth can be emotionally devastating as well as physically challenging to navigate. Most of us have either known someone who has been through a miscarriage, or perhaps we have experienced it ourselves.

If losing a baby has been part of your journey, find peace in knowing that Jesus cares so much about you, and he loves your child more than anyone. A miscarried child never dies; the precious baby goes straight into God's loving arms. Your child is fully alive and experiencing all the wonders of Heaven with Jesus forever.

Today, if you are grieving the loss of a child, lean into the comfort and peace that God's Spirit gives, and set your mind on the promise that you will be reunited with your child one day in Heaven. Hold on to the hope that one day you will forever experience the joy-filled, loving relationship with your child that you have longed for here on earth.

Prayer: *Dear Father, losing a child is a sorrow beyond words. I pray for those who have lost children and thank you for the day we will all be reunited, when we can spend eternity together in your presence.*

94

When I saw him, I fell at his feet. . . . Then he placed his right hand on me and said, "Do not be afraid. I am the First and the Last. I am the Living One; I was dead, and now look, I am alive forever and ever!"

Revelation 1:17–18

As the men watched, Jesus' appearance was transformed so that his face shone like the sun, and his clothes became as white as light.

Matthew 17:2 NLT

W HEN ASKED to describe what Jesus looked like, Mary Neal said,

My answer is very clear, even though it's nonsensical. I would say he looked like bottomless kindness and compassion. And those are not words that make sense, because those aren't words that we use visually—but that is what he looked like. It wasn't a matter of looking at someone and saying, "Oh, you know, brown hair and you know, whatever." He looked like bottomless kindness and compassion.

And in terms of his outward appearance, I would say the same thing as the other people I saw . . . a physicality. He had arms, legs; again, it's this filamentous robe exploding with love. . . . It was as though he was everything. He is everything.[1]

Dean also wrestled for the words to describe Jesus's appearance:

I was on my hands and knees as I looked into His face. How do I tell you what His face looks like? His face was as if it were liquid crystal glass made up of pure love, light, and life. From His face came the colors of the rainbow and colors I cannot describe inside His being. All these colors were part of Jesus and they were coming out from His being as the waves of the ocean come to the seashore. . . . I just wanted to praise Him forever.[2]

The Bible records Jesus's appearance as described by his disciples before and after his resurrection. During his ministry on earth, Scripture describes him being a man of stature, strength, and wisdom, as well as gentle, loving, and kind.

In Heaven, he is more glorious, beautiful, and powerful than we can even imagine. You will one day see him, fully alive in all of his glory and brilliance, shining with the light and love of God.

When you see Jesus in Heaven, you will be captivated by the pure love that embodies who he is. And even now, he wants you to feel his radiating presence every moment of every day as he shines his light and love upon you, his child.

Today, worship him as you focus on his loving presence and what it will be like to see him face-to-face in all of his brilliance one day. Let yourself freely receive the kindness, compassion, and love that he is giving you now.

> **Prayer**: *Dear Jesus, I praise you for your constant love and presence in my life. I can't wait to see you face-to-face in all your glory!*

95

God saved you by his grace when you believed. And you can't take credit for this; it is a gift from God. Salvation is not a reward for the good things we have done, so none of us can boast about it.

Ephesians 2:8–9 NLT

O NE THING NDErs RECOGNIZE is that you can't pretend or hide, cover up or mask anything. In the light of God's eyes, the truth about ourselves is fully known, and there's no one to blame, nowhere to hide, and no excuses to make. One day we will fully realize the truth even if we spent a lifetime fooling ourselves. The only thing left to do is take responsibility for it. And God wants us to do that now, so that we can be free of all pretenses. Then, with his help, we can grow into the people he intended.

Dutch researcher and cardiologist Dr. Pim van Lommel wrote about a patient who shared this after his NDE:

> I lingered at those incidents where I had trouble recognizing my responsibility until I was ready to accept it. To everybody I had ever hurt, intentionally or unintentionally, I wanted to explain why and express my sincerest apologies. Nobody condemned me, and at all times I felt this warm support. How could this support love me? Could it not see how naïve I had been in life? And that I had been motivated by ambition, selfishness, fear—and, yes—even by joy or euphoria? Fortunately, I also saw and felt all the wonderful, happy, rewarding, and joyful moments that my thoughts, words, and actions had given others (and thereby myself). Everything was shown simultaneously—my entire life![1]

Jeffrey Long observes that NDErs were typically the ones who judged themselves.[2] Maybe that's why Jesus said:

A good man brings good things out of the good stored up in him, and an evil man brings evil things out of the evil stored up in him. But I tell you that everyone will have to give account on the day of judgment for every empty word they have spoken. For *by your words* you will be acquitted, and *by your words* you will be condemned. (Matt. 12:35–37, italics mine)

One woman said, "I saw how selfish I was and how I would give anything to go back and change."[3] Another man recalls:

Next he showed me my life review. Every second from birth until death you will see and feel, and [you will] experience your emotions and others that you hurt, and feel their pain and emotions. What this is for is so you can see what kind of person you were and how you treated others from another vantage point, and you will be harder on yourself than anyone to judge you.[4]

God's love and compassion for us is not based on our good or bad deeds; they are free, unconditional gifts. Jesus did not come to condemn but to save. A natural response would be to allow his love and forgiveness to motivate us to love him and treat others the way he does.

When you understand the extent of his grace and mercy bestowed upon you, you cannot help but give that grace to others. Even though it is hard to forgive those who have wronged you, you are actually connecting to God's heart the most when you do forgive. And it frees you to live without resentment and anger toward others.

Today, think of ways you can give the love and grace of God to the people in your life, and freely give as God has given to you, regardless of how they respond. This will draw you close to the heart of God, you will grow to become more like him, and he will reward you.

Prayer: *Lord Jesus, thank you that I am unconditionally loved, and not condemned but saved by your grace. Help me to extend that same grace to others in my life.*

96

> But Jesus said, "Let the children come to me. Don't stop
> them! For the Kingdom of Heaven belongs to those who are
> like these children."
>
> Matthew 19:14 NLT

FOUR-YEAR-OLD COLTON BURPO was in the backseat as they passed the hospital where he'd almost died earlier that year. When Todd jokingly asked Colton if he wanted to go back, Colton blurted out that the angels sang to him there. When asked what songs they sang, he explained that they sang "Jesus Loves Me" and "Joshua Fought the Battle of Jericho." Todd and Sonja were shocked to hear their son claiming to have seen Jesus when he nearly died, and Todd asked where Colton met Jesus. Colton replied nonchalantly, "I was sitting in Jesus's lap."

As Todd and Sonja probed more, they discovered that Colton claimed he'd left his body, and while watching the doctor from up in the air, he could also see Todd in another room shouting at God for letting his son die and Sonja on the cell phone in the lobby. As more and more details came forth, details a four-year-old couldn't know, they started to believe Colton had actually experienced something real.

Days later, as Colton played with his X-Men action figures, Todd asked him what Jesus looked like. Colton set his toys down and looked up at Todd. "He has brown hair and he has hair on his face." Colton didn't yet know the word beard. "And his eyes . . . Oh, Dad, his eyes are so pretty!" As he said this, Colton looked as if he was enjoying a wonderful memory.

Every time Todd or Sonja saw a portrait of Jesus, they would ask Colton if that's what Jesus looked like. For over two years and hundreds of portraits, Colton always saw something wrong with every Jesus picture. Several years later, Todd saw a CNN special on artist prodigy Akiane Kramarik, who reported seeing Heaven when she was four years old. She described Heaven's amazing colors and Jesus, who was "very masculine, really strong and big. And his eyes are just beautiful." It struck Todd that two four-year-olds both mentioned all the colors of Heaven and the amazing eyes of Jesus. When Colton saw Akiane's *Prince of Peace* painting that night on CNN's website, he stared at the screen and declared, "Dad, that one's right!"[1]

A doctor and his wife came to our church after their three-year-old son almost died. At the time of the incident, neither of them had ever talked about God or Jesus, nor had their kids ever been to church. Yet as the son was being tucked into bed one night, he declared, "I want to run through the fields and play with Jesus again." His mother was surprised and kept asking who told him about Jesus (they surely hadn't!). He insisted that Jesus came and took him from the hospital, and "they ran and played in beautiful meadows together." Their son's experience was the catalyst that led both of them to faith.[2]

Maybe God is younger in heart than we tend to be. Jesus told us that Heaven belongs to the childlike ones. Children don't stress; they play, they enjoy, they explore, they trust. The world grooms us with worries, distractions, cynicism, and insecurities that hijack our innocence and our ability to notice the blessings of God's presence all around us.

Like these children who have experienced the presence of Jesus in Heaven, you too can confidently enjoy his presence in your life. Today, try to simply trust like a child would in the profound presence of Jesus—enjoying his creation and his fellowship, full of awe and wonder. Allow yourself to return to innocence, acknowledging his blessings and living in childlike freedom again.

Prayer: *Dear Heavenly Father, help me to have a confident, childlike trust that receives all the blessings of your presence. Return me to the wonder and joy of a child as I walk with my hand in your hand today.*

97

I no longer call you servants, because a servant does not know his master's business. Instead, I have called you friends, for everything that I learned from my Father I have made known to you.

John 15:15

Not only do people describe Jesus's awesome glory and palpable love, they describe him as a delight to be around. Some people can't imagine Jesus being the most joy-filled, fun person to be with, because they've never really contemplated what the Scriptures say. You'll never find a better best friend in the universe!

Colton Burpo said he sat on Jesus's lap. When he came back, he kept telling his father, Todd, how much Jesus loves the little children—most likely making sure that, as a pastor, Todd reminded people to prioritize the little ones.

Our doctor friend's young son said that after Jesus came to get him in the hospital, he was running and playing in the fields with Jesus. If Jesus invented play, adventure, fun—why wouldn't he enjoy it with us, just like we love to enjoy our own children's fun?

Richard noted how Jesus, as God, is also omnipresent. He can commune with the Father, play with little children, interact with groups of adults, and be with you and me personally in Heaven—simultaneously.

I saw Jesus walk up to the throne and disappear into the enfolding fire that surrounds the Being on the throne. Later, after leaving the throne room, I did see Jesus again from afar talking to different groups of people here and there. He seems to be everywhere. Children run to him continually, and he loves them all.[1]

Eben Alexander did not recognize Jesus (though he seemed to make a connection in church after his NDE), but he affirmed what Scripture says, and he feels people are mistaken when they think of God as impersonal: "Yes, God is behind the numbers, the perfection of the universe. . . . [But God] is 'human' as well—even more human than you and I are." Dr. Alexander observed that God empathizes with humans much more than we can possibly imagine.[2]

Imagine our powerful, Almighty God feeling like a close friend. Abraham trusted God and was called the "friend of God." The more you trust him, the deeper your friendship grows.

Jesus said to his disciples while on earth, "I no longer call you servants, because a servant does not know his master's business. Instead, I have called you friends" (John 15:15). John, the youngest disciple, called himself "the one Jesus loved," and during the Last Supper, John was kicked back, reclining on Jesus's chest like he would on an older brother (see John 13:22–25).

Jesus wants to enjoy your life with you, like a friend. It's truly awe-inspiring! He is the sovereign King of the Universe, more powerful than any ruler, yet he wants to be your friend.

Do something you enjoy today with your best friend Jesus. As you do something you love, thank him and talk with him about it. He created your ability to enjoy things, so realize he genuinely delights in doing them with you, just like two friends.

> **Prayer:** *Dear God, I am amazed that you, the God of the universe and the Creator of all things, would consider me your friend. Thank you for loving me and wanting to do life with me.*

98

Yet I am always with you; you hold me by my right hand.
You guide me with your counsel, and afterward you will take
me into glory. Whom have I in heaven but you? And earth
has nothing I desire besides you.

Psalm 73:23–25

AS DAVID SO ELOQUENTLY EXPRESSED in the Psalms, the presence of God is the longing of every human heart. There's no greater joy on earth that compares to intimacy with our Creator, the one who loves us most. Many NDErs describe the exhilarating joy they felt when they saw Jesus:

> I was so consumed by His presence that I dropped to my knees and looked up at Him. He is so glorious, so beautiful. All light inside of Light.[1] —Khalida

> I was filled with awe at His beautiful presence.[2] —Gary

> Seeing the majesty and indescribable beauty of the Lord made me speechless. . . . When I was in His presence, it was all I wanted.[3] —Samaa

> It's the pinnacle of everything there is. Of energy, of love especially, of warmth, of beauty.[4] —anonymous Dutchman

> The magnificence of this Person pierced me like a laser . . . all Power, all Wisdom, all Splendor, all Love. . . . Nothing mattered except to remain in this presence.[5] —Mickey

> Jesus is pure, unconditional kindness and compassion. And so the idea of being afraid never would've crossed my mind. It was so peaceful. So wonderful, so peaceful [that] I could have stayed there forever.[6] —Mary

The presence of God is something every human was created to experience, and we long for his presence in our lives to feel whole and complete. How exhilarating it will be to experience him in person one day!

Even in the waiting here on earth, God's presence is still with us. God has given us the Holy Spirit to fill us and empower us, and through his Spirit we can experience God's presence in our lives every moment of every day.

You can talk to God like you would a trusted friend, and he listens and cares about what is on your heart. James 4:8 says, "Come near to God and he will come near to you." As you face your trials and struggles, he will guide you. You can draw upon his presence for strength in your weakness and courage to persevere. He will give you hope for a new day and intercede for you in prayer.

This moment, draw near to God's presence and let his Spirit fill your mind and heart. Imagine the day when you will see his face and experience the pleasures of living with him for eternity.

Prayer: *Dear God, thank you that you are always with me. Your presence is continually guiding me and loving me through every moment of each day.*

99

For this world is not our permanent home; we are looking forward to a home yet to come.

Hebrews 13:14 NLT

The wall was made of jasper, and the city of pure gold, as pure as glass. The foundations of the city walls were decorated with every kind of precious stone. . . . The twelve gates were twelve pearls, each gate made of a single pearl.

Revelation 21:18–19, 21

CAPTAIN DALE BLACK describes getting ready to enter the gates of the city:

The wall to the city was not a single wall but rather a series of walls layered next to each other. The wall was made of three outer layers, three inner layers, and one higher wall in the center. . . . At its tallest point the wall was a couple hundred feet. And surprisingly, it was as thick as it was tall [Revelation 21 says 216 feet thick]. The wall was massive and stretched out to my left and right as far as I could see in both directions.

The outer wall was greenish in color with a hint of blue and a hint of black mingled within it. It was made entirely of translucent stones. Large multicolored stones were built into the base of the wall in layered rows.

The two angels that had escorted me there were still with me, moving me along. . . . I was eye-level with the base of the wall now and no longer hovering above it, but standing in front of an impressive opening. It was an archway that seemed to be approximately forty feet high and thirty to thirty-five feet wide.

A tall, majestic angelic being stood to the right side of the gate. . . . The entrance, or gateway, was opalescent in color, as if it had been made of pearls that had been liquefied, and then solidified onto the wall. The entrance was completely composed of this mesmerizing substance that also coated the entire inside of the opening as far as I could see. The ornamentation around the entrance included phenomenal detail. It was the most astounding sight I had ever seen.

As I basked in the beauty that adorned the gateway, I noticed large gold letters emblazoned above the opening. They seemed to quiver with life. The single line of letters formed an arch over the entrance. I didn't recognize the letters but knew the words were as important as any words could be. . . . I was filled with excited anticipation of entering that beautiful gate.

I was immersed in music, in light, and in love. Vibrant life permeated everything. All these weren't just around me, they were inside me. And it was wonderful, more wonderful than anything I had ever experienced. It felt as if I belonged there. I didn't want to leave. Ever. It was as if this was the place I had been searching all my life to find, and now I'd found it.[1]

The beauty and splendor of Heaven will be incredible to experience, and we get to live there forever! Imagine the wonder the first time your eyes behold the majesty of God's city. No longer will you have unmet desires or disappointments; all your longings will be satisfied.

On earth, we all have unmet longings and desires that can either lead us to discontentment or point us to the hope of Heaven and fulfillment found only in God. Blaise Pascal, a famous French philosopher, wisely said, "There is a God-shaped vacuum in the heart of every man which cannot be filled by any created thing, but only by God the Creator, made known through Jesus Christ."

As you allow God to fill your heart, he will satisfy more and more of your heart's desires. Ultimately, your soul's deepest longings will never be perfectly met here on earth, but they will be in Heaven. Today, let the hope of Heaven's splendor give you confidence to live for what matters now, knowing that one day all your desires will be satisfied, and you will be rewarded for making your life count while on earth.

Prayer: *Father, thank you for the glorious place you have prepared for me. I know that Heaven is where all my unmet longings will be finally satisfied.*

100

Jesus came to them and said, "All authority in heaven and on earth has been given to me. Therefore go and make disciples of all nations, baptizing them in the name of the Father and of the Son and of the Holy Spirit, and teaching them to obey everything I have commanded you. And surely I am with you always, to the very end of the age."

Matthew 28:18–20

FOURTEEN-YEAR-OLD HANNAH saw the joy of bringing others to Christ during her NDE:

[Jesus] asked me what I would like to do. Stay there or go back to Earth? . . .

I asked, "What was on Earth for me if I went back?" He told me he has like little presents for me strewn across this lifetime. . . . He told me about all the animals that he had for me. He told me about how much they loved me. I said, "Animals can love?" He said, "Yes, of course they can!"

He showed me my life in the future, if I were to go back. . . . I saw myself happy and laughing so much. I just wanted to be that happy, because I was so unhappy while I was on earth with the abuse and growing up being told that I was not going to heaven. I think my spirit was just crushed all the time. I didn't have a happy memory, not even one. I wanted to experience what that girl was that I was watching in front of me.

I saw myself get married and I was so happy to just be alive. I saw all the people I was going to save and bring to God. I just wanted everyone to feel the way I was feeling. The love was perfect and it was enough. . . . It was all I wanted and still want! After I saw how many people I was going to help bring to God, I knew I wanted to come back, but I was still scared to come back. I wasn't in a good home and I was being abused daily.

I broke my gaze with Jesus and started to look out onto Earth. I wanted him to come with me. . . . I loved him so much already. I never wanted him to leave me, ever! I turned back and looked at him. He was still smiling at me the same as he had the whole time. . . . He is the most beautiful man I have ever seen or will see again.

I got brave and asked if he would please come with me? He answered right away and said "Sure I'll go." I ran to Him and He to me and I said "YOU WILL?!" He was still smiling at me and wide-eyed with those magnificent deep blue eyes. He held me close again with my hands in his and close to his chest. I was so happy I can't express it at all in words.[1]

Jesus is always with you. When you believe that, it can give you confidence to love others enough to introduce them to the greatest Love in the universe. God wants all people to know and experience his love, but he won't force them. He commissions us to work with him to help others come to know him and receive his forgiveness, love, and leadership in their lives.

Only through God's mercy and grace does humanity have the power to overcome the evils of this world with his good. Because of this, the greatest good you can ever do is to help others come to know and receive the forgiveness Jesus offers and have access to the power of God working in their lives.

Today, ask God how he wants you to partner with him to bring others into his kingdom, starting now. Remember, as you reach out to others and share your faith with them, Jesus will be near to lead and guide you. He will love others through you.

Prayer: *Dear Lord, I want to share your forgiveness and grace with others. Guide me to share my faith with those you have prepared to hear your good news.*

Acknowledgments

A BOOK LIKE THIS is never a solo act, or in our case even a partnership, but rather a team effort. We are so grateful to the team of people responsible for making this devotional a reality. Not only has Jack Kuhatschek been a good friend, he has been a great editor on many of John's books. We are so grateful that Jack temporarily came out of retirement to cull through the stories and help us tremendously with this project. A big thanks to Chad Allen for getting the idea going and shepherding it through to completion. We are grateful for Dave Lewis, who got behind the idea of helping people daily "set their minds on heaven." Lindsey Spoolstra was so patient with us, and we so appreciate her excellence in editing the book. Thanks also to Brianne Dekker, Abby Van Wormer, Erin Bartels, and the rest of the Baker Books team for all their hard work in making this devotional beautiful and getting the word out. Thanks to Megan for not only sharing her story but also her support and prayers for this project. Thanks to all our friends who shared their stories to point people to God. We are truly grateful.

John and Kathy Burke

Notes

Day 1

1. Dale Black and Ken Gire, *Flight to Heaven: A Plane Crash . . . A Lone Survivor . . . A Journey to Heaven—and Back* (Minneapolis: Bethany House, 2010), 28–29, 98–106.

Day 2

1. This story is taken from an interview with Dr. Mary Neal by John Burke, October 2015, and Mary C. Neal, *To Heaven and Back: A Doctor's Extraordinary Account of Heaven, Angels, and Life Again: A True Story* (Colorado Springs: Waterbrook, 2012), Kindle ed., loc. 57–72.

Day 3

1. "Sarah W. Probable NDE," NDERF.org, accessed November 1, 2017, https://www.nderf.org/Experiences/1sarah_w_probable_nde.html.

Day 4

1. Steve Sjogren, *The Day I Died* (Bloomington, MN: Bethany House, 2006), Kindle ed., loc. 1126–33.

Day 5

1. "Julie H. Probable NDE," NDERF.org, accessed November 1, 2017, https://www.nderf.org/Experiences/1julie_h_probable_nde.html.

Day 6

1. Taken from Mally Cox-Chapman, *The Case for Heaven: Near-Death Experiences as Evidence of the Afterlife* (Windsor, CT: Tidemark, 2012), Kindle ed., loc. 433–94.

Day 7

1. The summary of Brad Barrows's NDE, including direct quotes, is from Kenneth Ring and Sharon Cooper, *Mindsight: Near-Death and Out-of-Body Experiences in the Blind* (Bloomington, IN: iUniverse, 2008), Kindle ed., loc. 18–21, 38–45.

Day 8

1. "Derry NDE," NDERF.org, accessed November 1, 2017, https://www.nderf.org/Archives/1derry_nde.html.

2. Black and Gire, *Flight to Heaven*, 109.

Day 9

1. Marvin J. Besteman and Lorilee Craker, *My Journey to Heaven: What I Saw and How It Changed My Life* (Grand Rapids: Baker, 2012), Kindle ed., loc. 12–14. Used by permission.

Day 10

1. Don Piper and Cecil Murphey, *90 Minutes in Heaven: A True Story of Death & Life* (Grand Rapids: Revell, 2006), Kindle ed., loc. 233–75.

Day 11

1. Neal, personal interview.

Day 12

1. Richard Sigmund, *My Time in Heaven* (New Kensington, PA: Whitaker House, 2009), Kindle ed., loc. 225–59.

Day 13

1. Jenny Sharkey, *Clinically Dead: I've Seen Heaven and Hell* (self-pub., CreateSpace, 2013), Kindle ed., loc. 16.
2. Sharkey, *Clinically Dead*, loc. 16–17.
3. Sharkey, *Clinically Dead*, loc. 25–31.

Day 14

1. Ring and Cooper, *Mindsight*, loc. 58.

Day 15

1. "Alexa H. NDE," NDERF.org, accessed November 1, 2017, https://

www.nderf.org/Experiences/1alexa_h_nde.html.

Day 16

1. Personal letter from Ann "Megan" Hagins, August 2, 2017.

Day 17

1. "Micki P. NDE," NDERF.org, accessed November 1, 2017, https://www.nderf.org/Archives/1micki_p_nde.html.

Day 18

1. Personal conversation with Don Piper, September 3, 2016.
2. Betty Malz, *My Glimpse of Eternity* (Bloomington, MN: Chosen, 2012), Kindle ed., loc. 97–98.
3. Black and Gire, *Flight to Heaven*, 102–3.

Day 19

1. "From Darkness into the Glorious Light," Global Evangelical Missionary Society, accessed May 5, 2015, http://www.gemsworld.org/Literature/For_Hindu_Friends/for_hindu_friends.html. For Jaya's explanation on where in the Vedas he came across these ideas, see *Imagine Heaven*, chapter 11, note 10.
2. Personal interview with Jaya Sankar, February 15, 2008.

Day 20

1. Taken from Todd Burpo, Sonja Burpo, and Colton Burpo, *Heaven Is for Real: A Little Boy's Astounding Story of His Trip to Heaven and Back* (Nashville: Thomas Nelson, 2010), Kindle ed., loc. 1339–48.
2. Burpo et al., *Heaven Is for Real*, loc. 1810–11.

3. Burpo et al., *Heaven Is for Real*, loc. 1442–81.

Day 21

1. Besteman and Craker, *My Journey to Heaven*, loc. 13, 75, 185.
2. Malz, *My Glimpse of Eternity*, loc. 925–37, 931–35. Used by permission.
3. Mary Neal, personal interview by John Burke, October 20, 2015.

Day 22

1. Adapted from Crystal McVea and Alex Tresniowski, *Waking Up in Heaven: A True Story of Brokenness, Heaven, and Life Again* (New York: Howard Books, 2013), Kindle ed., loc. 1257–1301, 2079–84.

Day 23

1. Michelle Wilson, "Nine Minutes in Heaven: Interview of Crystal McVea," *CBN* (video: 5:07 timestamp), accessed February 27, 2018, http://www1.cbn.com/700club /nine-minutes-heaven.
2. McVea and Tresniowski, *Waking Up in Heaven*, loc. 164–65.

Day 24

1. Howard Storm, personal interview by John Burke, October 30, 2015.
2. Howard Storm, *My Descent into Death: A Second Chance at Life* (New York: Doubleday, 2005), Kindle ed., loc. 27–28.

Day 25

1. Apart from that which is cited below, all quoted material in this chapter is from John Burke's interview with Howard Storm.

2. The last sentence of this paragraph is from Storm, *My Descent into Death*, loc. 35.

Day 26

1. George G. Ritchie and Elizabeth Sherrill, *Return from Tomorrow* (Grand Rapids: Chosen, 2007), Kindle edition, loc. 36–55. Used by permission.
2. Ritchie and Sherrill, *Return from Tomorrow*, loc. 20.
3. Quote from personal friend Michael Warden.

Day 27

1. Richard Eby, *Caught Up into Paradise* (Old Tappan, NJ: Revell, 1978), 204–5.

Day 28

1. Jeff Olsen, *I Knew Their Hearts: The Amazing True Story of Jeff Olsen's Journey Beyond the Veil to Learn the Silent Language of the Heart* (Springville, UT: Plain Sight Publishing, 2012), Kindle ed., loc. 528–57.

Day 29

1. "Eben Alexander: A Neurosurgeon's Journey through the Afterlife," YouTube video, August 27, 2014, https://www.youtube.com/watch?v =qbkgj5J91hE.
2. Eben Alexander III, *Proof of Heaven* (New York: Simon & Schuster, 2012), Kindle ed., loc. 8–9, 29–32, 38, 48–49, 143.

Day 30

1. Piper and Murphey, *90 Minutes in Heaven*, loc. 416–27.
2. Alexander, *Proof of Heaven*, loc. 45.

3. Sid Roth and Lonnie Lane, *Heaven Is Beyond Your Wildest Expectations: Ten True Stories of Experiencing Heaven* (Shippensburg, PA: Destiny Image, 2012), Kindle ed., loc. 78–79.

4. Black and Gire, *Flight to Heaven*, 102–3.

Day 31

1. Gary Wood, *A Place Called Heaven* (New Kensington, PA: Whitaker House, 2014), Kindle ed., loc. 305–14.

2. "Eben Alexander: A Neurosurgeon's Journey," YouTube video.

3. Pim van Lommel, *Consciousness Beyond Life: The Science of the Near-Death Experience* (New York: HarperCollins, 2010), Kindle ed., loc. 74.

4. "Ray K. NDE," NDERF.org, accessed November 1, 2017, https://www.nderf.org/Experiences/1ray_k_nde.html.

Day 32

1. Roth and Lane, *Heaven Is Beyond Your Wildest Expectations*, loc. 84–86.

2. Storm, interview.

Day 33

1. "Teresa C. NDE," NDERF.org, accessed November 1, 2017, https://www.nderf.org/Experiences/1teresa_c_nde.html.

Day 34

1. Adapted from "Jennifer V.'s NDE," NDERF.org, accessed November 1, 2017, http://www.nderf.org/NDERF/NDE_Experiences/jennifer_v_nde.htm.

2. Besteman and Craker, *My Journey to Heaven*, loc. 31.

3. Storm, *My Descent into Death*, loc. 406–26.

Day 35

1. Ring and Cooper, *Mindsight*, loc. 16.

2. Ring and Cooper, *Mindsight*, loc. 468–70.

3. "Brian T. NDE," NDERF.org, accessed November 1, 2017, https://www.nderf.org/Experiences/1brian_t_nde.html.

4. "Mother Teresa Quotes," accessed February 27, 2018, http://www.azquotes.com/quote/493313.

Day 36

1. "Leonard NDE," NDERF.org, accessed November 1, 2017, https://www.nderf.org/Experiences/1leonard_nde.html.

2. Ritchie and Sherrill, *Return from Tomorrow*, loc. 64.

3. "Terry E. NDE," NDERF.org, accessed November 1, 2017, https://www.nderf.org/Archives/1terry_e_nde.html.

4. "Julie H. Probable NDE," NDERF.org, accessed November 1, 2017, https://www.nderf.org/Experiences/1julie_h_probable_nde.html.

Day 37

1. Black and Gire, *Flight to Heaven*, 99–100.

2. J. Steve Miller, *Near-Death Experiences as Evidence for the Existence of God and Heaven: A Brief Introduction in Plain Language* (Acworth, GA: Wisdom Creek Press, 2012), Kindle ed., loc. 12.

Day 38

1. "Jedraine C. NDE," NDERF.org, accessed November 1, 2017, https://www.nderf.org/Experiences/1jedraine_c_nde.html.

Day 39

1. "Sarah W. Probable NDE," NDERF.org, accessed November 1, 2017, https://www.nderf.org/Experiences/1sarah_w_probable_nde.html.
2. Wood, *A Place Called Heaven*, loc. 414–27.

Day 40

1. "Mary NDE," NDERF.org, accessed November 1, 2017, https://www.nderf.org/Archives/1mary_nde.html.

Day 41

1. Ring and Cooper, *Mindsight*, loc. 942–43.
2. Neal, personal interview.

Day 42

1. Storm, *My Descent into Death*, loc. 38.
2. Alexander, *Proof of Heaven*, loc. 48.

Day 43

1. "Rene Hope Turner NDE," NDERF.org, accessed November 1, 2017, https://www.nderf.org/Experiences/1rene_hope_turner_nde.html.
2. Storm, *My Descent into Death*, loc. 398–402, 510–13.

Day 44

1. "DW NDE," NDERF.org, accessed November 1, 2017, https://www.nderf.org/Archives/1dw_nde.html.
2. Braxton, *In Heaven!*, loc. 535–44.
3. McVea and Tresniowski, *Waking Up in Heaven*, loc. 586–92.

Day 45

1. Akiane Kramarik and Foreli Kramarik, *Akiane: Her Life, Her Art, Her Poetry* (Nashville: Thomas Nelson, 2006), 7–12, 34, 37.

Day 46

1. Olsen, *I Knew Their Hearts*, loc. 1160–208.

Day 47

1. Dean Braxton, *In Heaven! Experiencing the Throne of God* (Chambersburg, PA: Divine Design Publishing, 2012), Kindle ed., loc. 728–1258.
2. Neal, personal interview.

Day 48

1. Wood, *A Place Called Heaven*, loc. 263–72.
2. Patrick Doucette, *Is Heaven for Real? Personal Stories of Visiting Heaven* (Kindle Publishers, 2013), Kindle ed., loc. 113–14.

Day 49

1. Rebecca Springer, *Intra Muros* (Elgin, IL: David C. Cook, 1898), 10, http://hopefaithprayer.com/books/IntraMuros-SearchableText.pdf.
2. Ed Gaulden, *Heaven: A Joyful Place* (n.p.: Ed Gaulden Publishing, 2013), Kindle ed., loc. 697–708.

Day 50

1. Ring and Cooper, *Mindsight*, loc. 36–37.
2. Braxton, *In Heaven!*, loc. 728–33.

Day 51

1. "Bruce NDE," NDERF.org, accessed November 1, 2017, https://www.nderf.org/Archives/1bruce_nde.html.

Day 52

1. Black and Gire, *Flight to Heaven*, 28–29, 98–106.

Day 53

1. Ring and Cooper, *Mindsight*, loc. 20, 44.

Day 54

1. Bill Wiese, *What Happens When I Die? True Stories of the Afterlife and What They T–ell Us about Eternity* (Lake Mary, FL: Charisma House, 2013), Kindle ed., loc. 59–60, 79–80.

Day 55

1. Braxton, *In Heaven!*, loc. 730–46.

Day 56

1. Wood, *A Place Called Heaven*, loc. 305–14.
2. Besteman and Craker, *My Journey to Heaven*, loc. 76–77.
3. Besteman and Craker, *My Journey to Heaven*, loc. 146.
4. Black and Gire, *Flight to Heaven*, 107–8.
5. Van Lommel, *Consciousness Beyond Life*, loc. 33.

Day 57

1. Malick, *10 Amazing Muslims Touched by God*, loc. 81, italics mine.
2. Michael Sabom, *Light and Death* (Grand Rapids: Zondervan, 2011), Kindle ed., loc. 1673–78, 1664–72, italics mine.
3. Nancy Botsford, *A Day in Hell* (Mustang, OK: Tate Publishing, 2010), Kindle ed., loc. 201–8, italics mine.
4. Sjogren, *The Day I Died*, loc. 255–59, 250–52, italics mine.
5. Thoene and Habib, *Face to Face with Jesus*, Kindle ed., loc. 2157–65, italics mine.
6. *Soul Revolution* by John Burke (Zondervan, 2008) guides you through a sixty-day experiment to learn to discern God's voice and stay connected to him every moment of each day.

Day 58

1. "Sarah W. Probable NDE," NDERF.org, accessed November 1, 2017, https://www.nderf.org/Experiences/1sarah_w_probable_nde.html.

Day 59

1. Neal, personal interview.
2. Neal, *To Heaven and Back*, loc. 57.

Day 60

1. Miller, *Near-Death Experiences*, loc. 12.

Day 61

1. Pat Johnson, personal letter to Kathy Burke, July 30, 2107.

Day 62

1. Taken from Burpo et al., *Heaven Is for Real*, loc. 1030–67, 1100–10.

2. Sigmund, *My Time in Heaven*, loc. 824–25.

3. Roth and Lane, *Heaven Is Beyond Your Wildest Expectations*, loc. 84–85.

4. Piper and Murphey, *90 Minutes in Heaven*, loc. 299–317.

Day 63

1. The synopsis of Jack's NDE, including direct quotes, are from Raymond Moody Jr., *Life after Life* (New York: HarperCollins, 2001), 96, 100–101.

Day 64

1. Sjogren, *The Day I Died*, loc. 280–308.

2. Lindi Roughton, personal interview by John Burke, January 20, 2015.

Day 65

1. Storm, *My Descent into Death*, loc. 36.

2. Storm, interview.

Day 66

1. Wood, *A Place Called Heaven*, loc. 226–62.

2. "Barbara J. NDE," NDERF.org, accessed, November 1, 2017, https://www.nderf.org/Experiences/1barbara_j_nde.html.

3. "Mark NDE," NDERF.org, accessed November 1, 2017, http://www.nderf.org/NDERF/NDE_Experiences/mark_nde.htm.

Day 67

1. Bodie Thoene and Samaa Habib, *Face to Face with Jesus: A Former Muslim's Extraordinary Journey to Heaven and Encounter with the God of Love* (Bloomington, MN: Chosen, 2014), 176–80.

Day 68

1. Sharkey, *Clinically Dead*, loc. 660–84.

Day 69

1. McVea and Tresniowski, *Waking Up in Heaven*, loc. 239–78.

2. Olsen, *I Knew Their Hearts*, loc. 484–87.

3. Piper and Murphey, *90 Minutes in Heaven*, loc. 387–91.

Day 70

1. Sam Amundson, personal interview by John Burke, October 2015.

Day 71

1. "Alexa H. NDE," NDERF.org, accessed November 1, 2017, https://www.nderf.org/Experiences/1alexa_h_nde.html.

2. Besteman and Craker, *My Journey to Heaven*, loc. 31.

3. McVea and Tresniowski, *Waking Up in Heaven*, loc. 574–85.

Day 72

1. "Katie A's NDE," NDERF.org, accessed November 1, 2017, http://www.nderf.org/NDERF/NDE_Experiences/katie_a_nde.htm.

Day 73

1. Black and Gire, *Flight to Heaven*, 109–10.

2. Piper and Murphey, *90 Minutes in Heaven*, loc. 416–27.

Day 74

1. Ritchie and Sherrill, *Return from Tomorrow*, loc. 80–83, italics in the original.

Day 75

1. Roth and Lane, *Heaven Is Beyond Your Wildest Expectations*, loc. 2–4.

Day 76

1. Sharkey, *Clinically Dead*, loc. 16.

Day 77

1. Faisal Malick, *10 Amazing Muslims Touched by God* (Shippensburg, PA: Destiny Image, 2012), Kindle ed., loc. 81–82.

Day 78

1. "Douglass D. NDE," NDERF.org, accessed November 1, 2017, https://www.nderf.org/Archives/1douglas_d_nde_3107.html.
2. "Douglass D. NDE."

Day 79

1. "Hazeliene M. NDE," NDERF.org, accessed November 1, 2017, http://www.nderf.org/NDERF/NDE_Experiences/hazeliene_m_nde.htm.
2. Neal, personal interview.

Day 80

1. Olsen, *I Knew Their Hearts*, loc. 484–87.
2. "Hafur NDE," NDERF.org, accessed November 1, 2017, https://www.nderf.org/Experiences/1hafur_nde.html.
3. McVea and Tresniowski, *Waking Up in Heaven*, loc. 2079–84.

Day 81

1. Cox-Chapman, *Case for Heaven*, loc. 414–22.
2. "Robin M. NDE," NDERF.org, accessed November 1, 2017, https://www.nderf.org/Experiences/1robin_m_nde.html.

Day 82

1. Besteman and Craker, *My Journey to Heaven*, loc. 185–86.
2. Sigmund, *My Time in Heaven*, loc. 1133–52, 1326.
3. Roth and Lane, *Heaven Is Beyond Your Wildest Expectations*, loc. 117–18.
4. Doucette, *Is Heaven for Real?*, loc. 157.

Day 83

1. Storm, personal interview.

Day 84

1. Neal, personal interview.
2. Springer, *Intra Muros*, 15.
3. Sharkey, *Clinically Dead*, loc. 619–26.
4. "Rene Hope Turner NDE," NDERF.org, accessed November 1, 2017, https://www.nderf.org/Experiences/1rene_hope_turner_nde.html.

Day 85

1. Thoene and Habib, *Face to Face with Jesus*, 2185–93.
2. Malick, *10 Amazing Muslims Touched by God*, loc. 82–83.
3. Ring and Cooper, *Mindsight*, loc. 35.
4. "Derry NDE," NDERF.org, accessed November 1, 2017, https://www.nderf.org/Archives/1derry_nde.html.

Day 86

1. Eby, *Caught Up into Paradise*, 203–4.
2. Roth and Lane, *Heaven Is Beyond Your Wildest Expectations*, loc. 149–50.

Day 87

1. Black and Gire, *Flight to Heaven*, 100, 104.
2. Alexander, *Proof of Heaven*, loc. 45–46.
3. Roth and Lane, *Heaven Is Beyond Your Wildest Expectations*, loc. 12–13.
4. Braxton, *In Heaven!*, loc. 561–64.

Day 88

1. Ritchie and Sherrill, *Return from Tomorrow*, loc. 36–55, 86, italics in the original.

Day 89

1. Besteman and Craker, *My Journey to Heaven*, loc. 55–57, 60–61, 65–66.
2. Besteman and Craker, *My Journey to Heaven*, loc. 56.
3. Besteman and Craker, *My Journey to Heaven*, loc. 116.

Day 90

1. Storm, personal interview.
2. Sharkey, *Clinically Dead*, loc. 552–67.

Day 91

1. Springer, *Intra Muros*, 3–7.
2. Black and Gire, *Flight to Heaven*, 28–29, 98–106.

Day 92

1. Ritchie and Sherrill, *Return from Tomorrow*, loc. 64–65.
2. Storm, personal interview.

Day 93

1. Personal letter from Ann "Megan" Hagins, September 2, 2017.
2. Besteman and Craker, *My Journey to Heaven*, loc. 56.

Day 94

1. Neal, personal interview.
2. Roth and Lane, *Heaven Is Beyond Your Wildest Expectations*, loc. 2–3.

Day 95

1. Van Lommel, *Consciousness Beyond Life*, loc. 207.
2. Long and Perry, *Evidence of the Afterlife*, loc. 113.
3. "Hillary H. NDE," NDERF.org, accessed November 1, 2017, https://www.nderf.org/Experiences/1hillary_h_nde.html.
4. "Ron A. NDE," NDERF.org, accessed November 1, 2017, https://www.nderf.org/Experiences/1ron_a_nde.html.

Day 96

1. Taken from Burpo et al., *Heaven Is for Real*, loc. 200–201, 1069–72.
2. Personal story told by Christy from Gateway Church about her son.

Day 97

1. Roth and Lane, *Heaven Is Beyond Your Wildest Expectations*, loc. 118.
2. Alexander, *Proof of Heaven*, loc. 85–86.

Day 98

1. Malick, *10 Amazing Muslims Touched by God*, loc. 81.
2. Wood, *A Place Called Heaven*, loc. 695.
3. Thoene and Habib, *Face to Face with Jesus*, loc. 2147–54, 2199.
4. Van Lommel, *Consciousness Beyond Life*, loc. 34.
5. Mickey Robinson, *Falling to Heaven* (Cedar Rapids, IA: Arrow, 2003), 97.
6. Neal, personal interview.

Day 99

1. Black and Gire, *Flight to Heaven*, 105–7.

Day 100

1. "Sarah W. Probable NDE," NDERF.org, accessed November 1, 2017, https://www.nderf.org/Experiences/1sarah_w_probable_nde.html.

John Burke is the *New York Times* bestselling author of *Imagine Heaven, No Perfect People Allowed, Soul Revolution*, and *Unshockable Love*. As an international speaker, John has addressed hundreds of thousands of people in twenty countries on topics of leadership and spiritual growth. He is founder and senior pastor of the multisite community of Gateway Church, Austin. Keep in touch at ImagineHeaven.net, and on social media @johnburkeofficial (Facebook and Instagram) and @imagineheavenbook (Facebook).

Kathy Burke cofounded Gateway Church in Austin and served on the staff for many years. Kathy has contributed to and edited *Imagine Heaven* and *No Perfect People Allowed*. She has worked in financial consulting and missions, and for twenty years as a home educator. Kathy is currently a freelance writer and editor. Find her on social media @kathycburke (Instagram) and Kathy Covington Burke and @imagineheavenbook (Facebook). The Burkes have two grown children and a son-in-law, and they live in Austin, Texas.

The **BESTSELLING BOOK**
That **STARTED** It All

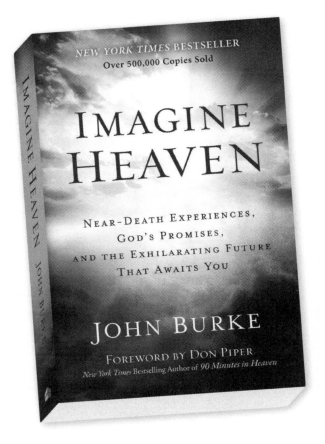